BRITAIN'S INLAND WA

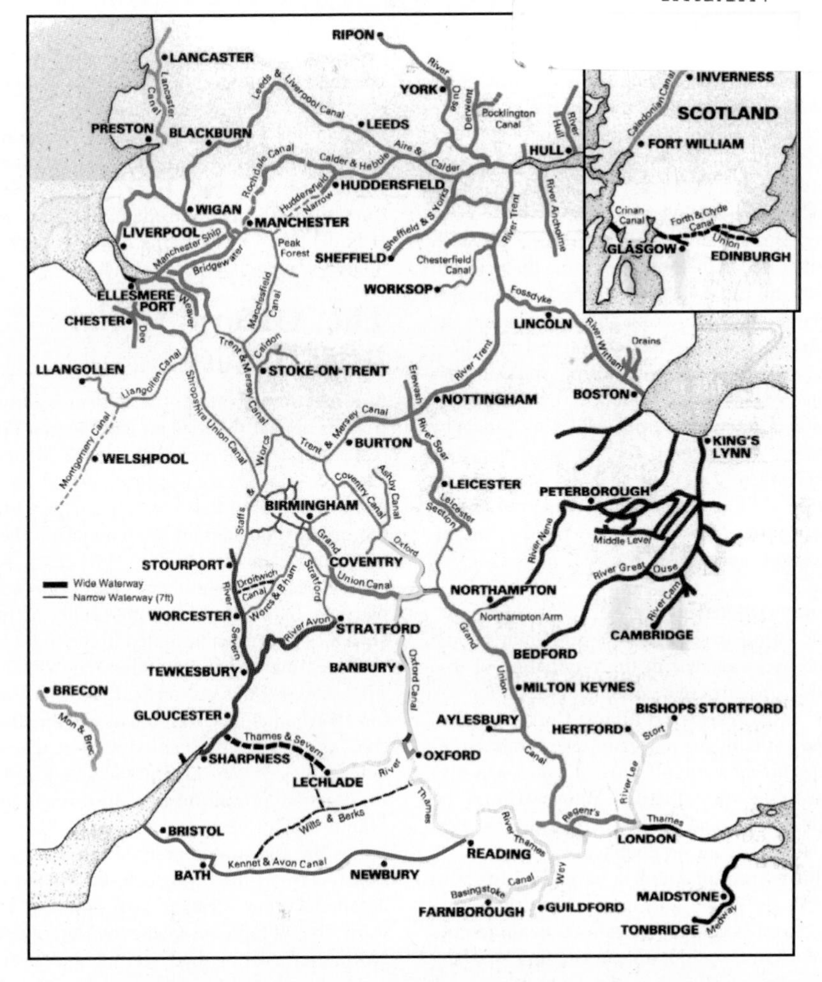

Published by Waterways World Ltd,

The Well House, High Street, Burton-on-Trent, Staffordshire DE14 1JQ, England

Researched and Edited by Euan Corrie

Maps and Artwork by Branch Out Design, Bretby, Burton-on-Trent

First Edition 2002

One of a series of guides covering the Inland Waterways of England and Wales

British Library Cataloguing in Publication Data

A Catalogue Record for this book is available from the British Library

ISBN 1 870002 76 8

Printed in England by Information Press, Eynsham

Introduction

This Guide covers the whole of the Oxford Canal from Hawkesbury Junction to the Thames at Oxford and in addition takes in a short length of the Grand Union Canal between Long Buckby and Napton. This new edition has been thoroughly revised and everything that the boater and towpath walker needs to know about this historic and beautiful canal should be found in its pages. It contains information about navigating the waterway, facilities for boating and shopping, and places of interest within walking distance of the canal. Moreover, towpath walkers and those who enjoy exploring canals by car are also catered for. So, whatever your interests are, we hope that you will find this guide useful. Have a good trip, remember the Country Code and enjoy discovering the Oxford Canal.

Acknowledgements

The editor is grateful to a great may people who have assisted in the production of this guide. In particular Marcus Potts undertook the initial research, Philippa Corrie acted as boat captain, car navigator, clerk and secretary on subsequent trips. Thanks are also due to the staff of British Waterways and the Aylesbury Canal Society's Launderette List is, as always, an invaluable aid.

Whilst strenuous efforts have been made to eliminate errors and ensure that the information this volume contains is as up to date and accurate as possible at the time of going to press, neither the editor nor Waterways World Ltd can accept any responsibility for any loss or injury resulting from its use. Inclusion of names and details of canalside companies, their services or facilities does not imply recommendation by the publishers. The editor would, however, be very grateful for any comments or corrections readers may forward to him at Waterways World Ltd, The Well House, High Street, Burton-on-Trent Staffordshire DE14 1JQ (Fax 01283 742957, email wwedit@wellhouse.easynet.co.uk).

The Oxford Canal – A Brief History

At a meeting of influential Midlands industrialists held at Warwick on 13th August 1767 it was agreed that a canal from the planned Trent & Mersey to Coventry would be of benefit to all, but that it was 'perhaps a little too early to consider an extension from there to Oxford'. Nevertheless in April of the following year, a preliminary discussion took place in Banbury on the possibility of just such a canal, and culminated in the first official meeting being held there in October 1768. £50,400 was subscribed, and the basis for a Parliamentary Bill drawn up. Finalised soon afterwards, it obtained its first reading before the year was out, but failed to gain the necessary approval until its third reading in March 1769.

James Brindley was appointed Engineer and, assisted by Samuel Simcock, he started his detailed survey straight away, putting forward the completed plans by August. By November cutting had started and over a mile near Hawkesbury was completed. Early in 1772 Brindley died, and Simcock - by this time his brother-in-law – took over as resident engineer.

Whilst strenuous efforts have been made to eliminate errors and ensure that the information this volume contains is as up to date and accurate as possible at the time of going to press, neither the editor nor Waterways World Ltd can accept any responsibility for any loss or injury resulting from its use.
The editor would, however, be very grateful for any comments or corrections readers may forward to him at Waterways World Ltd, The Well House, High Street, Burton on Trent Staffordshire DE14 1JQ
Fax 01283 742957, email wwedit@wellhouse.easynet.co.uk

1774 saw the canal reach Napton, forty miles from Oxford, but the company was already short of money. A second Act followed in 1775 to raise more money, and a year later the canal reached Fenny Compton. By November 1776, Banbury was only two miles away and Cropredy Wharf under construction. Then, 'to the sound of massed bands, tumultuous applause, and much rejoicing', the first load of coal arrived in Banbury on 30th March 1778.

The Oxford Canal north of Banbury was built to typical Brindley specifications – narrow locks with single top and double bottom gates, with the canal clinging closely to the contours of hill and valley. But it was to be another eight years before the canal progressed further, and when it did the underlying theme was 'thrift'! Locks were built deeper with single gates at both ends. Lift bridges, cheaper to build than stone bridges, were used wherever possible, and stretches of the river Cherwell were incorporated into the canal. On 1st January 1790 the bells rang out over Oxford as the band of the County Militia headed a fleet of boats into the new City Basin and the canal officially opened. By July, there existed a canal link from Manchester to Oxford and, at least for the time being, the Oxford Canal's prosperity was assured. Until the completion of the Grand Junction Canal, from Brentford to Braunston, the Oxford Canal, with the Thames, formed the through route from the Midlands to London.

The fascinating thing about the northern section of the Oxford Canal is that it was originally fourteen miles longer than it is today. In 1774 when the canal was completed between Napton and the Coventry Canal at Longford it was forty-three miles long, yet as the crow flies the distance is a mere sixteen miles! Up until the early years of the 19th century, with no competition, this tendency to faithfully follow the contours of the countryside mattered little, but completion of the

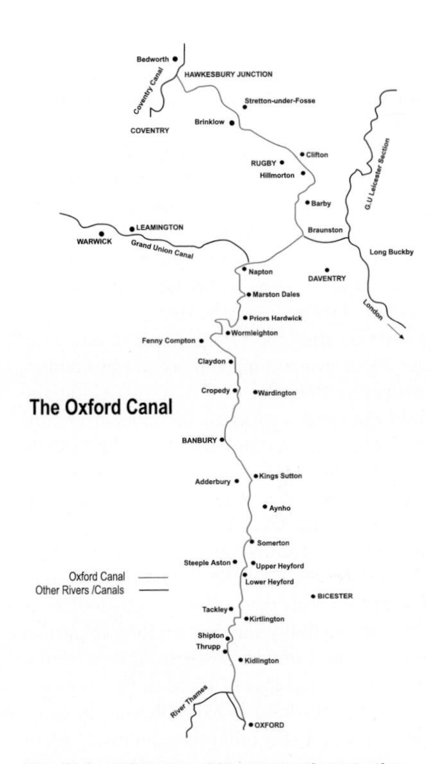

The Oxford Canal and its connections to the Thames and the waterways of the Midlands. Connecting sections of the Grand Union Canal around Braunston are included in this volume for the benefit of through travelers.

Grand Junction (later Grand Union) Canal as a rival route to London, and the promotion in 1826 of a new canal from Stratford-on-Avon to Braunston, resulted in the Oxford Canal Company awakening from its lethargy and surveying a much shorter route which was eventually completed five years later. The circuitous wanderings of the old main line were either left to silt up, or saw use as branch lines to village wharves.

Unluckily the 'shortenings' coincided with the advent of the Railway Age, and trade was soon being lost to the newer, faster mode of transport. By the 1860s, traffic was only 30% of its level twenty years before, though, ironically, one new source of revenue was the supply of canal water to the London & North Western Railway for the water troughs on the main line near Rugby.

As traffic began to transfer to railways from the boats, business at the canal wharves declined, tonnages fell steadily and receipts with them. The upheaval caused by the First World War badly affected the Oxford Canal and trade showed a further considerable decline during the war years.

However, after the Great War, the company set about overcoming the arrears of maintenance. In 1936 the Oxford Canal Company sold the canal's spacious terminal at Oxford to Lord Nuffield and the Nuffield College was eventually built on the site, thus the canal at Oxford now terminates abruptly in an aquatic cul-de-sac.

In 1934 the Braunston to Napton Junction section was widened by the Grand Union Canal Company who subsequently took over the responsibility for that section as part of their main London to Birmingham route.

After the initial loss of trade to the railways, traffic figures held remarkably well in comparison with many other navigations. Coal, of course, was the main reason for this, for carriage by narrowboat was still viable, and the Hawkesbury Junction to Braunston section remained busy with narrowboats carrying coal southwards from the Warwickshire and Leicestershire coalfields until the mid-1960s.

For many years the Oxford Canal remained the demesne of the horsedrawn boat, many of which were the colourful craft of the owner-boatmen known as the 'Number Ones'. Some of these boats were the most beautifully decorated of all canal craft, their colourful roses and castles contrasting with the grimey cargoes of coal which they frequently carried. In the 1930s only about one in thirty boats on the canal's southern section was mechanically powered, and horse-drawn boats continued to trade on this stretch long after they had disappeared from most other canals. The last of the owner-boatmen, Joseph Skinner, continued with his mule-drawn boat *Friendship* (now at the Boat Museum at Ellesmere Port) until 1959. The 'Number Ones' are immortalised in L.T.C. Rolt's famous book *Narrow Boat* which is recommended reading for all those who cruise the Oxford Canal today.

Despite its declining trade the Oxford continued to pay a dividend (one of the few canals that did) until nationalisation in 1947. Much of the remaining trade on the southern section was coal from the pits of the Coventry area carried to wharves at Banbury and Oxford, and some went to river wharves on the Thames via the Duke's Cut. Another regular traffic was tar from gas works at Oxford and Banbury. Trade finally ceased on the southern section of the Oxford Canal in the early 60s, by which time the canal was working at a deficit.

In 1948, following nationalisation, the Oxford Canal came under the control of the Docks & Inland Waterways Executive, then British Transport Waterways and, in 1963, the British Waterways Board, (now shortened to just British Waterways), under whose jurisdiction it is still maintained.

As commercial traffic disappeared from the waters of the Oxford Canal the southern section was threatened with closure, but the Inland Waterways Association held a rally of boats at Banbury in 1955. From that time pleasure boating began to grow. In the 1950s, holiday boating on canals was a novelty but the Oxford Canal a decade later was firmly established as a popular cruising waterway. In 1968 it was designated a 'Cruiseway' under the Transport Act of that year, since when pleasure traffic has continued to increase and the number of hire cruiser bases and marinas has multiplied. Today there are probably more pleasure craft on this canal than there ever were working boats, particularly at holiday periods and it is second only to the Llangollen in terms of popularity among pleasure boaters.

Navigating The Oxford Canal

Licences

Any boat using the waterways described in this guide will require a license. Addresses of all the authorities and organisations which can provide further information are listed on page 12

River Thames

Boat owners and hirers planning to enter or leave the Oxford Canal from the river at Oxford or via the Duke's Cut will require a licence for passage through the Thames. Registration forms and details of charges may be obtained from the Environment Agency at Reading. Transit Licences are also issued by the lock keepers at Osney (for craft joining the river via the Dukes Cut or at Oxford), at Teddington Lock (for boats joining the river from the tideway and at Blakes Lock for those entering from the Kennet & Avon Navigation). The Environment Agency and BW (see below) jointly offer a 'Gold Licence' for craft regularly using both authorities' waterways. But bear in mind that the Oxford Canal is a narrow beam waterway.

Oxford Canal

All craft, whether powered or unpowered, including canoes and dinghies, must have a British Waterways Boat Licence when navigating the Oxford Canal, or indeed, the rest of the connected canal system. Details of licensing are obtainable from the Waterway Managers at Braunston (01788 890666) or Fradley Junction (01283 790236) or from the Craft Licensing Department at British Waterways' Watford headquarters.

Some canal-based hire cruisers may carry a Thames as well as a British Waterways Licence, but the hirer should check this in advance with the boatyard proprietor if he wishes to navigate the river as well as the canal.

Navigation Notes

Stoppages

From time to time, particularly in the winter months (November-March), it may become necessary for BW to carry out maintenance work on the waterway. Alternatively, a dry spring or summer may result in restrictions due to shortage of water. Either of these circumstances may result in sections being closed or 'stopped'. Details of Stoppages are published monthly in *Waterways World* magazine. For unscheduled stoppages telephone Canalphone South (01923 201402). To obtain assistance or report emergencies outside office hours dial 0800 4799947 for Freephone Canals. Have details of the waterway and the nearest lock or bridge number or similar landmark ready.

Water

The Oxford Canal has been plagued throughout its history by shortage of water, and this is still a problem. The canal is shallow at the best of times, and the reservoirs fare little better, although remedial work is being undertaken by BW. So no matter what the prevailing weather conditions the canal will always be short of water - CONSERVE IT! Share locks, wait for oncoming boats if the lock is in their favour (even if it costs you five minutes, that's better than a dry pound!) and always ensure that all the gates and paddles are closed before leaving a lock unless an approaching boat obviously intends to use it.

Speed

There is a speed limit of 4mph on the canal and, usually, 6mph on rivers. Even this low speed is often too fast. Remember – an excessive wash or breaking wave causes bank erosion and damage to moored craft as well as being a general nuisance. If the wash from the stern starts to break up the banks EASE OFF, and you'll probably find that your speed in relation to terra-firma will increase anyway. Slow down when approaching or passing moored craft, other craft under way, locks, bridges, tunnels, engineering works and on bends. When the view ahead is obstructed, slow down, sound your horn and listen.

Rule of the Road

Craft meeting should steer to the right and pass each other left to left. If you do not intend to do this you must make it clear to the oncoming boat. When a vessel is being towed from the bank pass outside the vessel to avoid fouling the towing line – never pass between the towed vessel and the bank. Craft traveling with the current on rivers or tide-way have the right of way over those heading against the flow.

Depth

If you could see the canal drained of its water you'd be surprised how shallow it is, especially at the edges, the cross section being a shallow 'V' rather than 'U' shaped. Keep to the centre of the channel except when passing oncoming boats. This is particularly important on sections which have been concreted (see text accompanying maps for location). Give way to larger craft which require deeper water. You may find yourself aground if you have moved out of the centre channel to pass another boat. This is nothing to worry about. You should be able to reverse off, or push yourself off with your boat pole.

Flooding

Having pointed out the problems of water shortages, it may sound contradictory to raise the topic of flooding on the Oxford Canal but this too can be a hazard after heavy rain. At two points the river Cherwell and the canal join company; at Aynho and Shipton. If there has been a lot of rain these river sections rise dramatically and start to flow quite fiercely. When this happens boatyards will normally ask their hirers not to venture onto the river and private boaters would be advised to refrain from doing so as well.

Mooring

On rivers always moor with your bows pointing up-stream and allow sufficient slack on mooring lines to compensate for changes in level. The current is always faster through bridge arches and between bridge piers so do not attempt to turn up-stream of bridges. Always, unless specifically indicated to the contrary, moor against the towpath side of the canal. Steer your boat in bow first, put the engine into neutral and then pull the stern of your boat in with your rope. Keeping the propeller turning near to the bank could seriously damage the propeller and both the bed and bank of the canal. When pushing off again, ensure that the boat is well away from the bank before engaging forward gear.

• Do not moor too near bridges or locks so as to obstruct full size craft cruising the canal.
• Do not moor on bends or in winding holes.
• Do not moor in the short pounds of a flight of locks.
• Do not stretch ropes across towpaths where they will obstruct and endanger towpath users.

Safety First

Remember always that prevention is better than cure. Wear non-slip footwear and beware of slippery lock sides and gates in wet weather. Beware of low bridges – some of which are lower in the middle (sometimes with supporting girders) than at each end. Make sure that your crew is aware of the presence of a low bridge – especially those sitting on the cabin top. Before you enter a long tunnel, tell the crew to switch on the cabin lights (the cabin lights shining on the walls are useful to the helmsman). Ensure that torches are handy when entering tunnels and for use at night.

It is advisable to be able to swim when contemplating a holiday afloat. Non-swimmers and young children should wear life jackets. When walking along the side-decks use the handrails on the cabin top.

Picture: Robin Smithett

Building their canal south of Banbury the Oxford Canal Company were experiencing increasing financial difficulties. One legacy of this for modern boaters is the attractive lift bridges. These have limited clearance for your cabin and certainly no room for crew members on the roof or gunwales as the boat squeezes through the narrow opening.

Make sure that you know the position and method of operation of the fire extinguishers provided on the boat. Take a basic first aid kit with you including insect repellent. It is a good rule to spend the first night aboard making sure that you know where everything is, how emergency equipment works and reading the instructions or handbooks on essential equipment provided by the owner.

Tunnels

Canal craft should be equipped with a suitable headlamp for navigating tunnels which should be trained slightly to the right to avoid dazzling oncoming steerers in wide tunnels. Torches should also be carried. Go dead slow when approaching other craft but do not stop in tunnels except in an emergency.

There is only one tunnel on the Oxford Canal, Newbold Tunnel 250 yards long, which has twin towpaths. This was built during the modernisation scheme of the early 19th century when the other tunnel, at Fenny Compton, was opened out. Unpowered craft are prohibited from the tunnel.

Bridges

Height

Several bridges have little headroom between cabin roof and brickwork. Boaters, particularly those with roof-top passengers, chimneys and tall pipes, are advised to look well ahead and play it safe rather than sorry!

Lift bridges

Part of the charm of the Oxford Canal is generated by the many and varied bridges that cross it, not least of which are the famous wooden lift bridges, approximately 22 of which still exist. Few of the lift bridges open to the vertical, so keep your boat well away from the 'hinge' and make sure that the cabin is clear; nobody should be on the cabin roof! Aim to clear the towpath-side abutments by an inch or so, the cabin top should then clear the bridge. Many of the lift bridges are heavy and have no means of being secured down. Do not allow children to operate a lift bridge – they will often be unable to move it at all! Always have at least one heavyish person sitting on the balance beam until the boat is clear. Occasionally these bridges have been 'modernised' and require your lock windlass to operate the hydraulic pump with which they are raised.

Usually these are merely farmers' access bridges. If you find one down, then the farmer is probably using it, so leave it as you find it. Where a bridge is part of a thoroughfare keep a look-out for approaching vehicles and try not to cause a hold-up for too long. Use your common sense, and if you are in any doubt ask someone – you'll appear a lot less foolish in the end!

When approaching these bridges, never allow anyone to stand at the bows of the boat near to where the cabin might hit the bridge – several tons of boat traveling at up to 4mph could easily crush them between boat and bridge. Never attempt to get off the boat onto the deck of a moveable bridge, this has proved fatal several times.

Note: Do not stand on the roof of the boat or anywhere along the gunwale nearest the bridge deck when passing under lift bridges and never attempt to get off the boat on to the bridge deck.

BW Sanitary Station keys

It is essential to have at least one of these, Yale type keys, on board to gain access to Sanitary Stations and water points. Keys are available for sale direct from British Waterways (see under Useful addresses) and from most boat yards and marinas.

Mileage

Hawkesbury to Braunston: 23
Braunston to Napton: 5
Napton to Oxford: 49

Locks

Lock dimensions. In canal parlance, the Oxford is known as a narrow canal, meaning that the waterway, and more particularly the locks, were built to take the traditional English narrowboat. Today, the lock dimensions are:

Length - up to 72ft (21.9m)
Beam – up to 7ft (2.13m)
Headroom 7ft (2.13m)
Draught – up to 3ft (0.91m)

Number of locks – Hawkesbury to Braunston: 4
Braunston to Oxford: 39

Lock Operation

The golden rule is never waste water. The lock drill described below should be followed systematically.

The basic principle of lock operation is that water never passes straight through a lock. It comes in from the top and stays in, or goes out through the bottom without any following it from the top. If you liken the lock itself to a kitchen sink – the top end to the tap and the bottom to the plug – don't turn the tap on until the plug is in, and don't pull the plug out until the tap is off.

Lock-keepers On the river Thames lock-keepers are usually on hand to direct traffic and operate the lock. This is the exception; lock operation on canals is usually undertaken by the boat crew. At busy spots lock-keepers may be available to assist and regulate traffic. They may ask you to share a lock with another boat or wait whilst another boat comes through the other way. Obey their instructions but do not necessarily expect that they will do the work for you – that's part of the fun of your holiday.

Staircase Locks Await you in other parts of the country but will not be encountered on the Oxford Canal.

Picture: Dusty Miller

How to Operate Locks

A windlass is usually required to fit the paddle spindles of manually operated locks. These will usually be provided on the boat and have two holes of different sizes to take the spindle's squared end. Take care to use the correct sized hole on the spindle as a bad fit is dangerous since the windlass may fly off. In direct contravention of the recommendation of its own paddle gearing committee BW has fitted a mixture of sizes of spindles at numerous locks so constant attention is needed. Do not leave the windlass on the spindle when not winding the paddle up or down – make sure the pawl is in place to stop the paddle falling and remove the windlass so that it cannot fly round if the catch slips.

Those of the crew who operate the paddles must remember that the noise of the engine and rushing water will prevent people on the boat hearing their instructions or them hearing shouts of panic. Those ashore are responsible for keeping an eye on the boat all the time that the lock is filling or emptying to see that it continues to rise or fall steadily. If there is any doubt shut all the paddles quickly and then stop to think and check if the boat or its ropes and fenders are catching on any part of the lock or other boats. Particularly check that the stem fender does not catch under the top gate or its handrails when going up hill. Boats sharing locks, which is a good way to save water, must lie beside or ahead and astern of one another, never twisted across each other at bow or stern. Like that they will jam as the level alters.

(1) Going Uphill – Lock Empty

Check that top gates are shut and paddles closed.

Illustation: Dusty Miller

Open the top gate paddles when their outlets in the gates are submerged (where applicable). Some locks have only gate paddles and greater care is needed here to avoid flooding the fore end when going up hill by opening these too much too rapidly.
When the lock is full open the top gates.
Leave the lock. Close the top gates and all paddles.

Enter the lock and drive the boat to the far end where there will be less turbulence as the lock fills.
Close the bottom gates. See that the bottom gate paddles are closed.
Open top ground paddles (where applicable). Water from these will pass under the boat to the other end of the chamber and hold the boat against the top gate or cill.
Ropes are not usually required to hold a boat steady in narrow locks but will often be a good idea in bigger chambers. A spring running slightly astern from the fore end may be best with some tension being maintained by keeping the engine running in forward gear. Do not tie knots in any rope used in locks, they will jam when it is necessary to adjust the length of line as the water rises or falls and leave the boat hanging in mid air or sunk. Do not try to hold a rope as the lock fills either; take a couple of turns round a cleat or bollard and the extra friction thus gained will help prevent the boat dragging the rope through your hand causing nasty burns as it does so.
In most wide beam locks, such as those on the Kennet & Avon or Grand Union canals, where two or more narrowboats will fit alongside one another, a less turbulent ascent for a single boat, will result from drawing the top ground paddle on the same side as the boat first. The water will usually pass beneath the boat and help to hold it steadily against the wall.

(2) Going Uphill – Lock Full

Check that there is no boat approaching from above the lock which could save water by descending as you empty the lock for your boat to enter.
If not, close the top gates. See that the top gate and ground paddles are closed.
Open the bottom paddles.
When the lock is empty open the bottom gates and close the bottom gate paddles. Proceed as (1) above.

(3) Going Downhill – Lock Full

Enter the lock and drive the boat to the far end where it will be well clear of the cill near the top gates as the water drops.
Close the top gates. See that the top gate paddles and ground paddles are closed.
Open the bottom gate paddles.
When lock is empty open the bottom gates.
Leave the lock. Close all bottom paddles and gates.

(4) Going Downhill – Lock Empty

Check that there is no boat approaching from below the lock which could save water by ascending as you fill the lock for your boat.
Close the bottom gates. See that the bottom gate paddles are closed.
Open the ground paddles.
Open the top gate paddles when submerged (where applicable).
When the lock is full, open the top gates. Proceed as (3) above.

Before leaving a lock see that all paddles are fully and securely closed. On canals it is important to shut the exit gates as well; failure to do so may result in serious flooding of property, stranding of craft through loss of water from the pound above, and possible flooding of craft when the pound is refilled.

It is easiest to pick up lock crew at the lock mouth which saves approaching the shallow canal margins where you may run aground. But in all situations where crew are joining or leaving even a slowly moving boat make them get on or off at the stern. Should they slip they will then get wet after the boat has passed and not fall in where it will pass over them or crush them against a wall. At the stern the steerer is also at hand to put the engine out of gear quickly and assist.

Beyond The Towpath

This publication is intended primarily as a guide to the canal but it also includes information on some of the places of interest near the canal. More detailed information can be obtained from local tourist offices. (See the text accompanying the maps and pages 12 and 13 for details of Tourist Offices).

Walking The Oxford Canal

Although canal towpaths are not usually Public Rights of Way, the public is now encouraged to make use of these excellent long-distance footpaths. Some very good canalside walks may be enjoyed by combining lengths of towpaths with the official footpaths and bridleways marked on the appropriate OS Landranger 1:50,000 maps covering the area. Many of these tracks and byways are also marked on the maps in this guide. Work has been done to improve the towpath along the Oxford Canal which now forms part of a waymarked long distance route. Where fences or gates cross the path walkers should leave them as they find them. Stout footwear is essential.

Though 'lock-wheeling' is as much part of today's boating as it was in the days of working boats, it is an offence to cycle along the towpath without a permit. These are obtainable from British Waterways local Waterway Manager's office or from BW's Head Office. There are some lengths of towpath where cycling is not permitted, details of which will be sent to applicants along with their free permit which must be displayed on handlebars at all times. Cyclists without a permit are liable to a fine.

Similarly, it is an offence to ride a horse along the towpath.

General

Always respect the pleasure of other waterway users and the life of the countryside generally. Do not litter or pollute the waterways and always observe the Country Code -

- Guard against fire risks.
- Fasten all gates.
- Keep dogs under proper control.
- Keep to the paths across farm land.
- Avoid damaging fences, hedges and walls.
- Protect wildlife, wild plants and trees.
- Go carefully on country roads.

Bibliography

The Oxford Canal by Hugh J. Compton. Published by David & Charles, 1976. The history of the Oxford Canal from the passing of the first Act in 1769 to the present day.

Narrow Boat by L. T. C. Rolt. Originally published by Eyre & Spottiswoode, 1944. New edition republished by Alan Sutton, Gloucester, 1994. Unequalled in canal literature. A 1939 voyage through the canals of the Midlands beginning and ending on the Oxford Canal.

The Flower of Gloster by E. Temple-Thurston. First published in 1911, this is an account of a journey by horse-drawn narrowboat during the canal's heyday. Reprint published by Alan Sutton.

A History of Oxfordshire by Mary Jessup. Published by Phillimore, 1975.
A History of Banbury by William Potts. Reprint of 1958 issue by the Gulliver Press, Banbury, 1978.
Ordnance Survey Landranger 1:50,000 maps 140, 151 and 152 cover the route of the canal and its immediate connecting waterways.

Video

The Oxford Canal – a tour of the canal and its surrounding countryside, produced by Waterways World.

Maps and Charts

GEOprojects map of the Oxford Canal – fold-out boater's map.
Ordnance Survey maps (Landranger Series) 1:50,000 scale: sheets 140 Leicester & Coventry, 151 Stratford-upon-Avon, 152 Northampton & Milton Keynes and 164 Oxford.
Note: British Waterways publish a range of information leaflets – copies of these may be obtained (free) from BW's Braunston and Fradley offices – see under Useful Addresses.

Guides to adjoining canals

This guide links up with others in the series at:
1. Napton Junction - *The Waterways World Guide to the Grand Union (North)*. (New edition currently in preparation.)
2. Braunston Turn - *The Waterways World Guide to the Grand Union (North)*, *The Waterways World Guide to the Coventry Ashby & Oxford (North)* Canals, including the Birmingham & Fazeley and *The Waterways World Guide to the Grand Union (Leicester Section)*.
(New editions currently in preparation.)
3. Hawkesbury Junction - *The Waterways World Guide to the Coventry Ashby & Oxford (North) Canals*, including the Birmingham & Fazeley.

Other guides in this series:

Trent & Mersey Canal (including the Caldon Canal), Grand Union (South), Kennet & Avon Canal, Llangollen Canal (including the Montgomery Canal), Shropshire Union Canal, Staffs & Worcs Canal.

All are available from: Waterways World Ltd, The Well House, High Street, Burton upon Trent, Staffordshire DE14 1JQ (01283 742950).

Useful Addresses

The Environment Agency, Thames Region, Kings Meadow House, Kings Meadow Road, Reading RG1 8DQ (0118 9535000, www.environment-agency.gov.uk). Recorded navigation information 0118 9535620.

British Waterways

Waterway Managers: Oxford Canal to Bridge 9; central Grand Union Canal, including the Leicester Section: British Waterways, The Stop House, Braunston, Northamptonshire NN11 7JQ (01788 890666, Fax 01788 890222, christine.styles@britishwaterways.co.uk).
Bridge 9 to Hawkesbury Junction: British Waterways, Fradley Junction, Alrewas, Burton-on-Trent, Staffordshire DE13 7DN (01283 790236, Fax 01283 791411).
British Waterways (Headquarters and Craft Licensing); Willow Grange, Church Road, Watford, Hertfordshire WD17 4QA (01923 226422).BW's web site is at www.britishwaterways.co.uk

Tourist Information

Oxford: Tourist Information Centre, The Old School, Gloucester Green, Oxford OX1 2DA (01865 726871).
Banbury: Tourist Information Centre, 8 Horse Fair, Banbury (01295 259855).
Oxfordshire County Museum, Fletcher's House, Park Street, Woodstock (01993 811456).

Rugby: Tourist Information Centre, 4 Lawrence Sheriff Street, Rugby, Warwickshire CV22 5EJ (01788 533839).

Inland Waterways Association PO Box 114, Rickmansworth, Hertfordshire WD3 1ZY (01923 711114, Fax 01923 897000; email iwa@waterways.org.uk; web site waterways.org.uk/index.htm).
Association of Pleasure Craft Operators, Parkland House, Audley Avenue, Newport, Shropshire TF10 7BX. (01952 813572, Fax 01952 820363; email apco@bmif.co.uk, web site www.bmif.co.uk).
Canal Society: Coventry Canal Society, 28 Kempley, Coventry, Warwickshire CV2 5LP (024 7645 7771; email coventrycanalsociety@yahoo.com, web site www.covcanalsoc.co.uk (Moorings on the Oxford Canal near Hawkesbury Junction)

Hire Boat Companies operating on the Oxford Canal

Club Line Cruisers, Swan Lane Wharf, Swan Lane, Stoke Heath, Coventry CV2 4QN (01203 258864). (Based on the Coventry Canal.)
Rose Narrowboats, Fosse Way, Stretton under Fosse, Nr Rugby Warwickshire CV23 0PU (01788 832449 www.rosenarrowboats.co.uk).
Willow Wren Cruising Holidays, Rugby Wharf, Consul Road, Rugby CV21 1PB (01788 562183).
Clifton Cruisers, Clifton Wharf, Clifton-on-Dunsmore, Rugby, Warwickshire CV23 ODG (01788 543570, Fax 01788 579799, email cliftoncruisers@hotmail.com, web site www.cliftoncruisers.com).
Avalon Narrowboat Co, 11 Coneygar Road, Quenington, Gloucestershire GL7 5BY (Tel & Fax 01285 750567, www.avalonboats.com) Operate from Enslow Wharf.
Union Canal Carriers Ltd, The Pump House, Canal Side, Little Braunston, Northamptonshire, NN11 7HJ (01788 890784). (Based on the Grand Union Canal.)
Calcutt Boats Ltd, Calcutt Top Lock, Stockton Rugby CV47 8HX (01926 813757 email boats@calcutt.demon.co.uk, web site www.calcuttboats.com). (Based on the Grand Union Canal.)
Napton Narrowboats, Napton Marina, Stockton, Rugby CV47 8HX (01926 813644).
Black Prince Holidays, Napton Marina, Stockton, Rugby. (01527 575115).
Anglo-Welsh Waterway Holidays have several bases, that on the Oxford Canal is at Lower Heyford. Their headquarters is at 5 Pritchard Street, Bristol BS82 8HR (0117 924 1200, Fax 0117 924 0202, email bookings@anglowelsh.co.uk web site www.anglowelsh.co.uk)
Oxfordshire Narrowboats Ltd, Canal Wharf, Station Road, Lower Heyford, Bicester, Oxfordshire OX25 5PD (01869 40348).
College Cruisers, Combe Road Wharf, Oxford, OX2 6BL (01865 54343, www.collegecruisers.com).

Public Transport

Buses – National Express (Nationwide service) (08705 80 80 80).

Most comprehensive answers are available from Warwickshire Traveline 01926 414140. The main operators are: Stagecoach Oxford 01865 772250, Stagecoach Midland Red 01788 535555, Stagecoach United Counties 01604 702112, AM Cars 0500 212225 and Geoff Amos Coaches 01327 260522,

Train information is best obtained from the National Enquiry Number (08457 484950).

Hawkesbury Junction

Hawkesbury Junction is the meeting place of the Oxford and Coventry canals. An attractive iron bridge spans the famous hairpin junction linking the two canals and, adjacent to the junction, is an old pumphouse which has been the subject of restoration proposals in recent years. Formerly a popular mooring place for the working boat people, Hawkesbury Junction (known to the boatmen as Sutton's Stop) has undergone a considerable amount of improvement work in recent years. Some of this endures, despite the encroachment of new housing estates, to make the junction as attractive an area today as it has been an interesting and busy one in the past.

The Greyhound pub overlooks the junction while, a short walk away, in Blackhorse Road, is the Boat Inn, a traditional pub which has family connections with the canals going back over many years.

There is a chemical toilet disposal facility but no public toilets here.

Bridges 1–4

The Stop Lock is very shallow, having been intended originally to prevent the free passage of water between the two canals. There is ample space for casual mooring on any of

Picture: Robin Smithett

Occasional working boats still call at Hawkesbury Jiunction, indeed some now load at the wharf on the Coventry Canal there, since the demise of local waterside collieries. Ivor Batchelor is seen here bringing his well laden *Mountbatten* round from the Coventry Canal towards the Stop Lock at the northern end of the Oxford Canal. Beyond the attractive towpath bridge the Coventry Canal extends (left) towards its eponymous city and (right) to Atherstone and the Brimingham & Fazeley or Trent & Mersey canals.

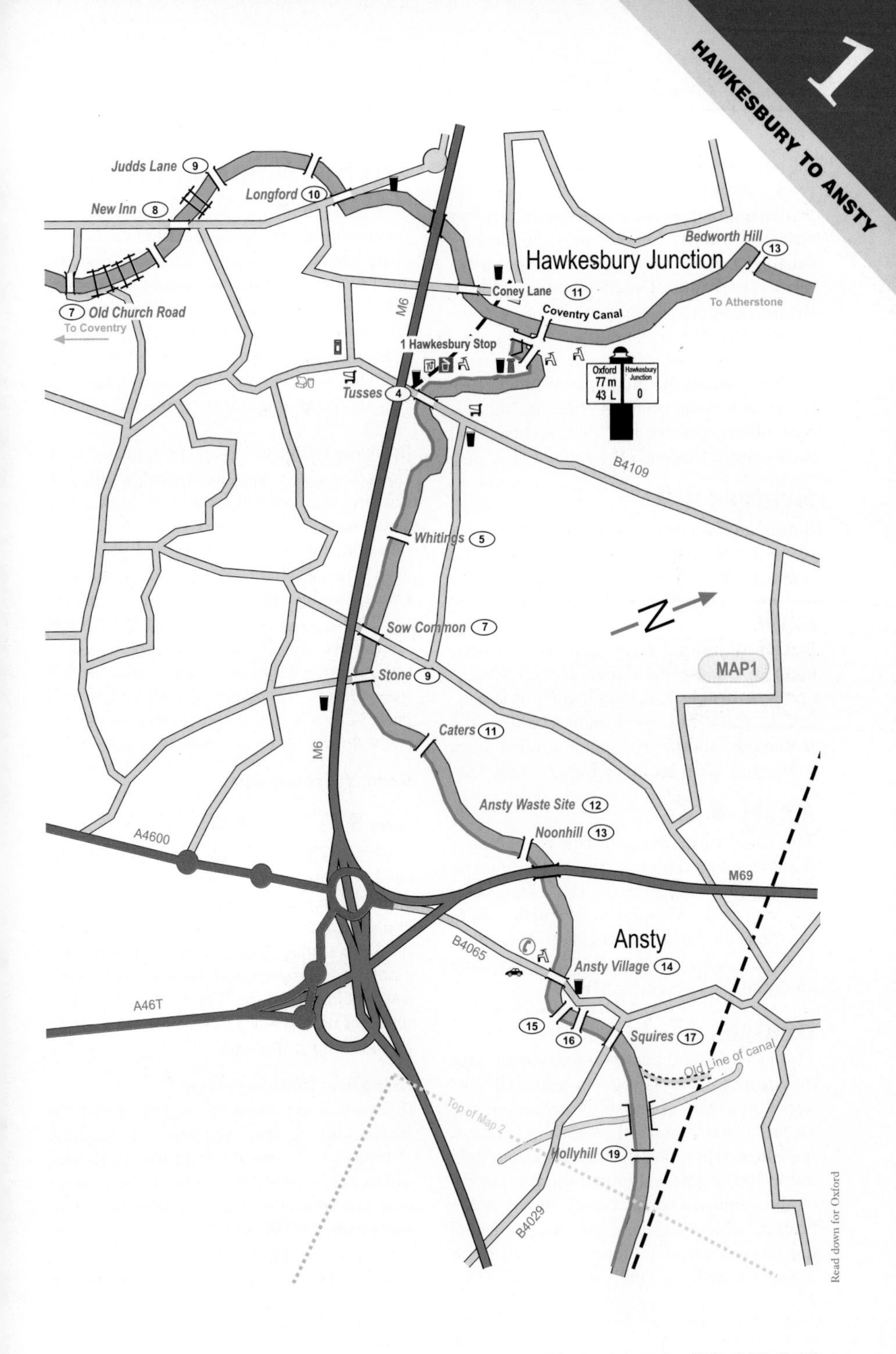
Judds Lane 9
Longford 10
New Inn 8
Bedworth Hill 13
Hawkesbury Junction
Coney Lane 11
To Atherstone
7 Old Church Road
To Coventry
M6
Coventry Canal
1 Hawkesbury Stop
Oxford
77 m
43 L
Hawkesbury Junction
0
Tusses 4
B4109
Whitings 5
Sow Common 7
MAP1
Stone 9
Caters 11
M6
Ansty Waste Site 12
Noonhill 13
A4600
M69
Ansty
B4065
Ansty Village 14
A46T
15
16
Squires 17
Old Line of canal
Top of Map 2
Hollyhill 19
B4029
Read down for Oxford

the approaches to the junction. Pylons converge overhead and the towpath is bordered by the landscaped site of a redundant power station formerly served by coal-carrying canal boats which delivered to a huge stockpile on the offside. The Elephant & Castle by Bridge 4 offers snacks and light refreshments and has a large, pleasant garden adjoining the towpath. About 1/2 mile from Bridge 4, under the motorway at Alderman's Green is a useful group of shops including a post office, grocery and newsagents, plus, further on, a fish and chip shop.

Bridges 4-9

Running beside the M6 motorway, the canal passes the Wyken Arm, which was part of the original line of the canal and now put to good use as moorings by the Coventry Canal Society.

British Waterways have split the management of the Oxford Canal, apparently randomly at Bridge 9, north of which it is controlled from Fradley Junction whilst the remainder, southwards, is controlled from Braunston. (See useful addresses, page 12.)

Ansty

The canal runs past a row of houses on a shallow embankment with the imposing Georgian frontage of Ansty Hall overlooking the waterway. The Rose & Castle offers moorings for patrons at its canalside gardens and play area. Bar meals are available lunchtimes and evenings daily.

Bridges 17-27

The canal shares a lofty embankment with the main Euston–Glasgow electrified railway. Three types of transport meet where the M6 motorway crosses the canal and railway. A shallow depression in a neighbouring field marks the original and much winding course of the original Oxford Canal. Many of the bridges which are now missing from the numbering sequence were on these, no longer navigable, sections of the canal.

Stretton Stop and Brinklow

An even older transport route than the canal – the Roman Fosse Way – crosses at Bridge 30. The canal narrows at the site of a former toll house and the present day home of Rose Narrowboats. The old Stretton Arm, used for moorings, gives access to the wharf where Brinklow Boat Services specialise in restoration and reprodiuction of traditional craft.

Brinklow village is about 15 minutes walk along the Fosse Way from Bridge 30. The remains of an ancient motte and bailey castle are situated behind the parish church of St John the Baptist. The long and pleasantly open village street has several pubs and shops, including a grocers, post office, newsagent, pharmacy, plus a pottery, fish and chip shop and Chinese takeaway. Brinklow was formerly situated on the original winding course of the Oxford Canal and several place names in the village, such as 'Dockyard' remind us of its former waterway activity.

Rose Narrowboats

(01788 832449 www.rosenarrowboats.co.uk). Hire craft, solid fuel, servicing and repairs, moorings, slipway, canalia, chandlery, Honda outboards and generators and all types of 230 volt electrical systems, boatbuilding, fiting out, painting and repairs, gift shop. 12 seater narrowboat for daily hire. The well stocked shop makes it unnecessary to walk all the way into Brinklow for provisions.

Brinklow Boat Services

is located at Stretton Wharf, which is reached up the arm from Stretton Stop, one of those which remains from the shortening works of the 1830s. It specialises in restoration and reproduction of traditional craft. Steelwork (01788 833331), fitting out and other wood work (01788 833789) as well as painting and decoration of ex-working craft

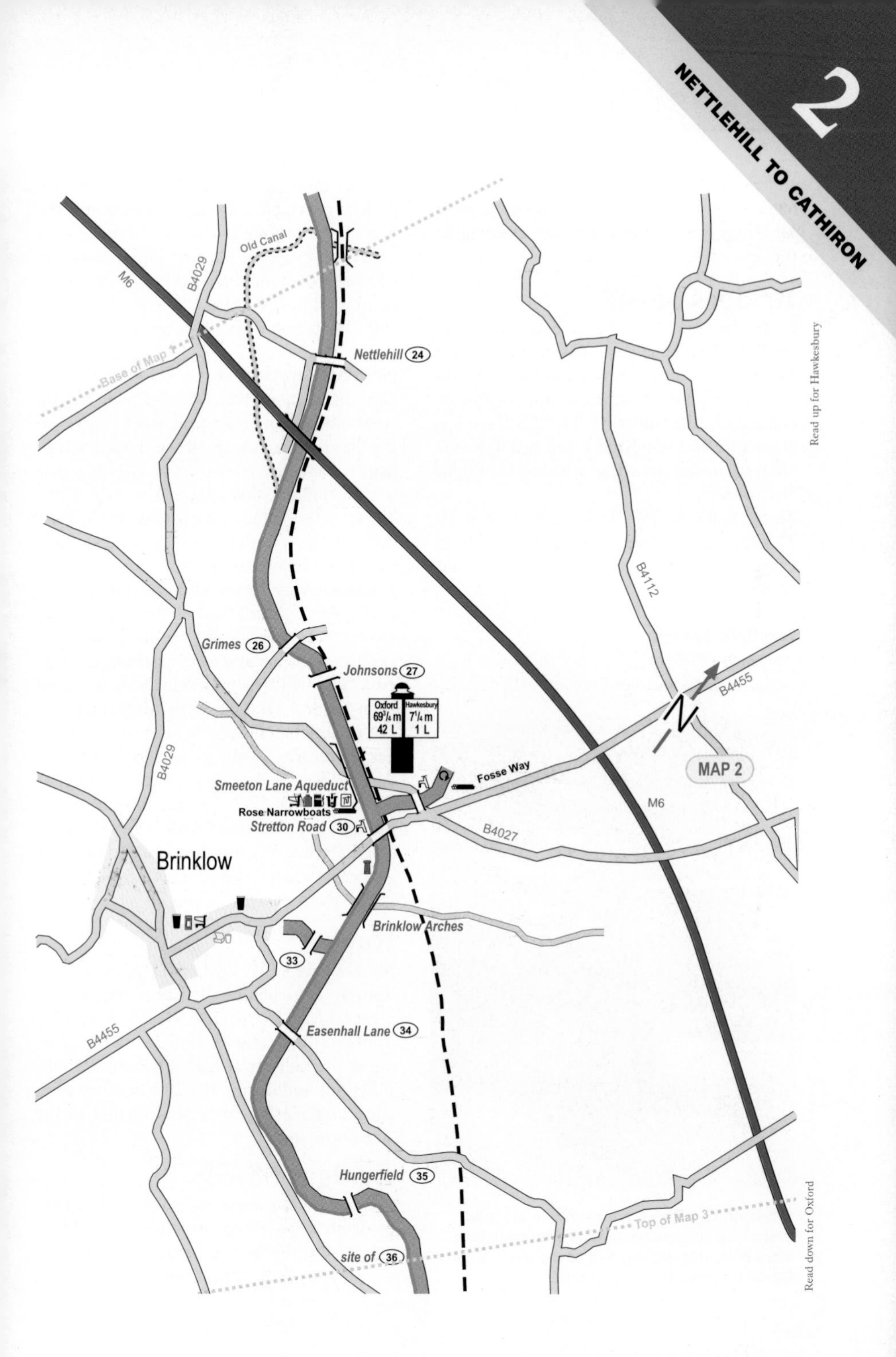
NETTLEHILL TO CATHIRON
2
Old Canal
M6
B4029
Base of Map 1
Nettlehill 24
Grimes 26
Johnsons 27
Oxford 69¾ m 42 L
Hawkesbury 7¼ m 1 L
B4112
B4455
MAP 2
Fosse Way
Smeeton Lane Aqueduct
Rose Narrowboats
Stretton Road 30
B4027
Brinklow
Brinklow Arches
33
B4455
Easenhall Lane 34
Hungerfield 35
Top of Map 3
site of 36
Read up for Hawkesbury
Read down for Oxford

and reproduction of these boats are undertaken by a skilled partnership of enthusiasts. Moorings, water point, craneage and engine repairs.

Bridges 30–48

Embankments and cuttings betray this section's 1829 vintage; the older, more tortuous route going off beneath handsome cast-iron roving bridges in a series of unnavigable or completely filled-in arms. The broad sweeps of pasture and woodland come as a welcome contrast to the industrial excesses of Rugby or Coventry.

Terry Yates (01788 569140). By Bridge 48. Mechanical repairs and refits, welding, crane, hull blacking sterngear and tube manufacturers. Full machine shop facilities.

Newbold Tunnel

250 yards. The tunnel we use today was built in the early 1830s to replace an earlier one on the old route of the canal. Adjacent to the parish church of St. Botolph you can still see one of the former portals at the edge of a field where only a shallow dip reveals the course of the older canal. The newer tunnel is unusual in that it has a towpath on either side. There is just room for two craft to pass.

Picture: Euan Corrie

Hillmorton Locks were included in the modernisation scheme when duplicate chambers were built. Interesting, and easily used, Oxford Canal Co paddle gear survives.

Newbold-on-Avon

Now little more than a suburb of Rugby, Newbold was once an important centre on the Oxford Canal with all the usually attendant wharves warehouses and stables and it is still an interesting spot.

Three pubs vie for your custom. At the Boat you can play 'Northampton' or table skittles, the beer is Davenports, and bar meals are available every lunch and evening. At the Barley Mow there's real ale, meals and bar snacks every lunch and evening, pool and skittles in the bar and a large garden and play area. The Old Crown, a short walk downhill from Bridge 51, is also an M&B pub and serves lunch-time bar snacks. The village has a number of shops including a launderette, fish & chip shop, butcher and general store/PO. The parish church of St. Botolph is just a short walk from the canal, and a Methodist Church is situated near the shops. Extensive visitor moorings are available between bridges 50 and 51.

Rugby

All services, EC Wed, MD Mon & Sat. Tourist Information 4 Lawrence Sheriff Street, CV22 5EJ (01788 533839, Fax 01788 534979). Rugby mushroomed with the coming of the railways (Charles Dickens' Mugby Junction) and during the 20th century electrical engineering has added further to the size of the town.

Bridges 58–59

A development along the valley of the river Swift includes a large supermarket and DIY stores, and the Bell & Barge – a Toby Grill restaurant. Walk into Brownsover housing

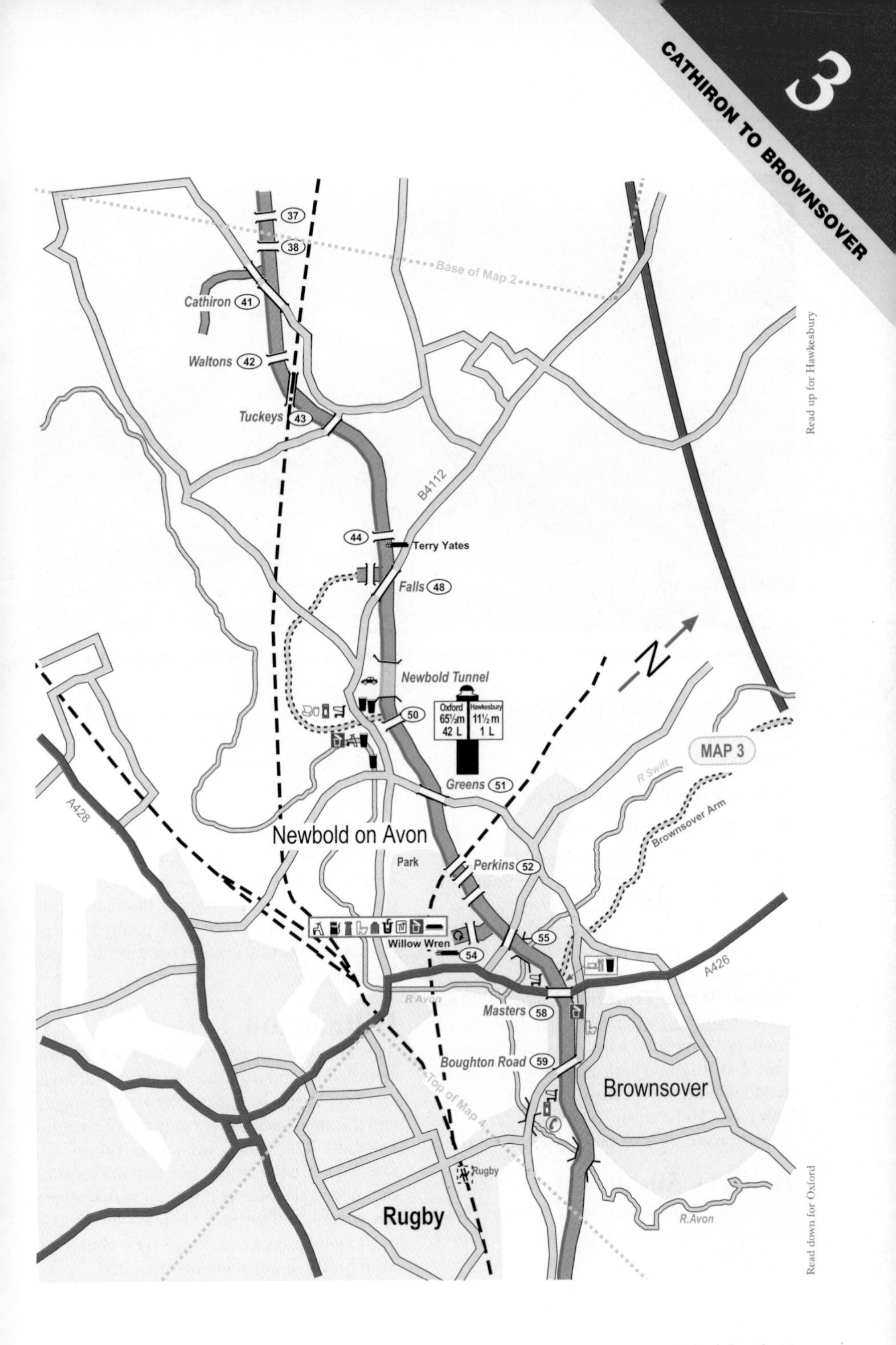

Read up for Hawkesbury

Read down for Oxford

Picture: Euan Corrie

Empty working boats tied up at Newbold Wharf are passed by loaded craft emerging from Newbold Tunnel.

estate for the modern Merrie Monk pub and a parade of shops including off licence and chippie.

Willow Wren Cruising Holidays (01788 562183, Fax 01788 540540, www.willowwren.co.uk). Closed Sundays. Large hire craft, pumpout, D, W, Elsan, RD, CG, moorings, toilets, showers, wetdock, craneage, Boat Safety Inspections, engine repairs, boat fitting and painting.

Willow Wren Training (01788 569183, email training@willowwren.co.uk). Closed Sundays. Associated with the above, based at Unit 2 at Rugby Wharf, provides training in handling craft to RYA Boatmaster and Inland Waterway Helmsman certificate levels as well as providing RYA diesel engine courses.

Bridges 50-69

The canal loops Rugby on a hillside above the valley of the river Avon which becomes navigable just above Strafford-on-Avon. Between Bridges 58 and 59 a little park has been provided on the off-side with picnic tables. Bridge 59 offers the best access into the town centre and there are suburban shops nearby,

Clifton Cruisers (01788) 543570, www.cliftoncruisers.com). Hire craft (including day hire) moorings, pumpout, servicing & repairs (including call outs), gift shop, traditional painted ware, provisions, boat fitting and painting and boat handling courses.

Hillmorton

The suburban sprawl of Rugby which has engulfed Hillmorton is thankfully hidden and kept at bay by the railway embankment, and the small canal-side community remains unspoilt. The house adjoining Bridge 71 used to be the New Inn but the only nearby pub now is the Stag & Pheasant which offers bar snacks, and the only shop left locally is a news agents in Lower Street. The church of St. John the Baptist adjoins the canal.

Picture: Euan Corrie

Unseen by many boaters, the aqueduct which carries the canal over the former Leicester main road at Rugby has been attractively restored.

The former British Waterways yard is the headquarters of their Watenway Environment Services, Architects and Landscape Architects, which helps to explain why the locks and towpath are so well maintained. The three locks are in pairs – an improvement carried out in 1840 to cater for increased traffic, and still beneficial in the busy summer months. Note the surviving, substantial cross-paddle gear which allowed water to pass between the adjacent lock chambers. Use of this allowed up to half of each lock full to be saved since adescending boat's water half filled the paired lock for an ascending boat. Unfortunately this gear is no longer operable.

Hillmorton Boat Services (01788 578661). Pump Out, repairs & servicing, boat painting, signwriting and fitting out including gas fitting to CORGI standards.

Canal Bridge Stores occupy part of the former maintenance yard and provides supplies and snacks as well as guides and souveniers daily between 8.30 am and 8.30pm.

Bridges 72–74

The myriad transmitting masts of Rugby radio station fill the eastern horizon, looking very pretty at night. The Old Royal Oak by Bridge 73 serves meals at lunch time and in the evening Mons–Sats and all day on

Sundays. (Booking is advisable for Sunday Lunch 01788 561401). Children and families welcome.

Blue Haven Marine (01788 540149) is next to the Royal Oak and provides perminant moorings, craneage as well as repairing boats and their engines.

Bridges 74–85

You cruise two lengthy straights dating from the 1830 improvements, and for a short period you are in Northamptonshire. The cutting between Bridges 83 and 84 is quite spooky, bats fly about at dusk and we wouldn't recommend mooring for the night!

Willoughby

Coal. On the A45 main road there is a cafe and two filling stations. In the village itself, about a further half mile, is the Rose pub, offering home cooked food, and a Post Office-cum-newsagents. The abandoned railway was formerly the Great Central Railway's main line, the last such main line railway to be built in Britain and one of the longest lines to be closed in the 1960s.

Bridges 85–90

A rolling pastoral landscape filled with sheep grazing to the water's edge. The uneven bumps in many of the fields are remnants of the medieval 'ridge and furrow' method of farming.

Braunston

The main line of the Oxford Canal skirts the northern edge of the famous canal village of Braunston, passing under the iron roving Bridge 94, and moving out into open country.

Braunston Branch: Bridge 91–Butchers Bridge

Boats, some of them on permanent moorings, line the towpath between the bridge and the toll house. Remains of the original stop lock which separated the two former rival canals can be seen just before the entrance to Braunston Marina. A fine Horseley Ironworks roving bridge crosses the arm, erected here during the improvement programme of the 1830s. The next bridge, Butcher's, is the first on the Grand Union and offers the easiest route up to the village.

Braunston village originally overlooked one of the Oxford Canal's meandering loops, up the Leam valley. Before the construction of the Grand Junction Canal (now part of the Grand Union) the older canal's line passed under the present A45 road twice, and through what is now the roving bridge over the entrance to Braunston Marina. Outside the Stop House (now British Waterways' Manager's Office, see page 12) by the entrance to the marina a Stop Lock was later provided to keep the Grand Junction Canal's water from flowing freely into the Oxford Canal. This was removed during the Grand Union's modernisation scheme in the early 1930s. Continuing into the marina and through the site of the present covered wet dock the route to Oxford crossed under the A45 again and followed the 325ft contour, generally south westwards, to pass through the later London & North Western Railway embankment. No bridge was provided beneath the railway since the canal loop had been disused for some years before the railway's construction. The canal continued its wanderings south and then westwards towards Wolfhampcote village. Parts of these loops may be traced on the ground, especially in wet weather. South of Wolfhampcote the channel approached close to the much later embankment of the now closed Great Cental main line and again under the LNWR branch as the canal again turned north. Close to Wolfhampcote Hall a surprisingly shallow 33-yard tunnel was provided under the lane before a watered section leads to the present canal alongside Bridge 97. The old line headed straight across the route of the

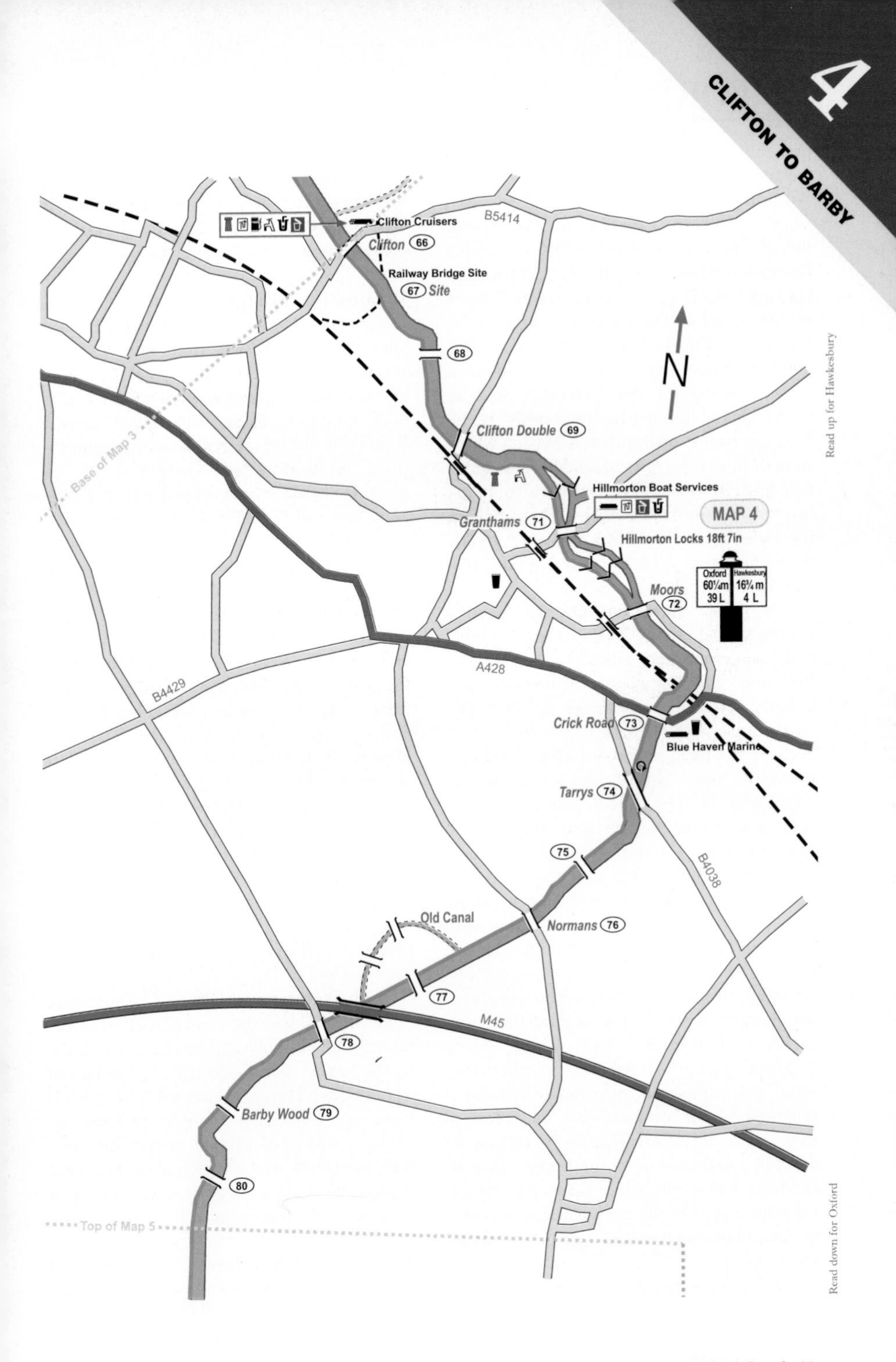
Clifton Cruisers
B5414
Clifton 66
Railway Bridge Site
67 Site
68
N
Clifton Double 69
Base of Map 3
Hillmorton Boat Services
MAP 4
Granthams 71
Hillmorton Locks 18ft 7in
Oxford 60¼m 39 L
Hawkesbury 16¾m 4 L
Moors 72
A428
B4429
Crick Road 73
Blue Haven Marine
Tarrys 74
75
B4038
Old Canal
Normans 76
77
M45
78
Barby Wood 79
80
Top of Map 5
Read up for Hawkesbury
Read down for Oxford

present canal looping round to rejoin it beyond Bridge 98.

With the opening of the Grand Junction Canal in 1805 the canal beyond the present marina entrance became the Oxford Canal's Braunston Branch with the Grand Junction starting from Butcher's Bridge, which bears number plate 1. The canal from here to the top of Long Buckby Locks is included in this guide book for completeness and as an aid to those heading for the Leicester Section. Alongside the first few hundred yards are the mooring basins of Braunston Marina which were built as reservoirs to hold lockage water run down Braunston Locks. Instead of being lost to the Oxford Canal this was returned up the locks by steam pumps housed in buildings which now accommodate Union Canal Carriers.

For over 200 years Braunston has been a bustling canal centre. Boats have been built and maintained here since the canals were first dug, and supporting businesses have congregated along the banks to serve the needs of passing boatmen.

Perhaps the most famous of all Braunston's boatyards was that of Nurser Brothers. Founded in 1878 by William Nurser, the yard became renowned for the boatbuilding skills of his two sons, Charles and Frank, who continued to work the firm after their father's death. Frank, the painter in the partnership, was also an excellent teacher of his craft and there are still pupils of the 'Nurser School' working today.

As well as boatbuilding, Braunston was also a major trade centre and several of the large carrying companies had yards here. Pickfords opened a depot soon after the canal was completed, but transferred their business to the railways early on, closing their yard in 1847. Fellows, Morton & Clayton, surely the most renowned of canal carriers, had a major transhipment depot here and many of their original warehouses, docks and offices remain as part of the marina complex.

When Nurser's closed in 1941 their business was bought by the Samuel Barlow Coal Co., who continued carrying until their boats, in turn, were taken over by Blue Line in 1963. It was Blue Line which first developed the boatyard and reservoirs as a marina.

Braunston village boasts a windmill, though it has lost its sails, and the tall church spire beckons boatmen from afar. A search through the churchyard will reveal the graves of many boating families. There are excellent facilities along the main street: Braunston Village Stores, known to generations of boaters as 'Gurney's' (01788 890334) should satisfy most needs and larger orders can be delivered to boats. It also has a cash machine. There's a wide range of shops, and a fish & chip shop. Of the pubs: the Wheatsheaf is a friendly 'local' pub always willing to serve snacks to hungry boaters, with skittles, pool table and weekend live music. The Old Plough at the top of the path from Butcher's Bridge, senves Ansells and home made meals at lunch times and evenings and has a garden. The Mill House, by the canal has a restaurant. It serves real ale, has a children's room, garden and moorings for patrons. The Braunston Fryer, at the top of the High Street provides takeaways on Wednesday–Saturday evenings and at lunchtime on Fridays and Saturdays.

All the many boatyards and facilities are to be found on the Braunston Branch of the Oxford Canal and on the Grand Union.

British Waterways' Office for the Oxford Canal and the central section of the Grand Union, including the Leicester Line in the former toll house (these days known as 'The Stop House, see page 12) is open on weekdays from 9am to 5pm (4.30pm on Fridays) and from 12noon to 4pm on summer weekends. It hosts regularly changing exhibitions and can provide a wide range of waterway information as well as gifts.

Midland Chandlers (Braunston) (01788 891401). A large showroom opposite

Picture: Robin Smithett

A narrowboat heads off the Oxford Canal's Braunston Branch towards the main line to Napton at Braunston Turn.

'The Turn' displaying traditional boat fittings, chandlery and painted ware, solid fuel stoves etc.

Ivor & Mel Batchelor are usually to be found close to the junction aboard their Admiral class working boats *Mountbatten* and *Jellicoe* from which they sell a variety of solid fuels, diesel and Elsan fluid. They will deliver larger orders locally (07885 651926).

Braunston Marina
(01788 891373, Fax 01788 891436). Open daily at least from 9am to 5pm. Launderette, pumpout, recycling, chandlery, moorings, painting, repairs & servicing (including call outs), slipway, craneage, and covered wet dock, CORGI gas fitting, Boat Safety Scheme Inspections, boat sales. Open daily. This marina provides a comprehensive range of services, mainly through the activities of the dozen or so independent businesses based around the site.

DB Boatfitting, Braunston Marina, (01788 891727, www.dbboatfitting.co.uk) fit out, paint and decorate craft.

Merlin Narrowboats, Braunston Marina (01788 891750, Fax 01788 577440, www.braunston.com) engine installations, electrics (230v specialist), CORGI gas fitting and signwriting.

Peter Nichols, Braunston Marina Trade Centre, (01788 891823, Fax 01788 899109, www.steelboats.com) builds qualty steel narrowboats, wide beam craft and sea going sailing vessels.

Barbara Ripley is based aboard her narrowboat at Braunston Marina (01788 890205) and produces hand made boaters' costumes, bonnets, spider's web belts (ready made or as DIY kits), hats, pottery and costume dolls.

Sab Signs (Sheila A. Bassett) Braunston Marina, (07747 805465) carry out signwriting and narrowboat artwork.

Shana, Braunston Marina (01327 877301) produces boat furnishings.

David Thomas, Braunston Marina (01788 891181) builds narrowboats.

Tradline Rope & Fenders, Braunston Marina (01788 891761, Fax 01788 899097, www.tradline.co.uk) can produce all types of fenders (particularly hand made traditional rope varieties) for narrowboats and large commercial craft and supply ropes, including steel, and a vast range of rigging equipment.

Those in need of further services or in search of a mooring closer to the village centre may wish to continue towards the botttom lock along the first few yards of the Grand Union Canal. Winding is possible in the second entrance to the former reservoirs.

Union Canal Carriers. Bottom Lock (01788 890784, Fax 01788 891950). M, pumpout, repairs & servicing, including call outs, drydock boatfitting. Hire craft, including day hire, camping narrowboats with or without crew. Courses leading to the acquisition of Royal Yaghting Association Helmsman's certificates are also offered.

Braunston Boats Ltd Bottom Lock (01788 891079) slipway to 70ft, boatbuilding and repairs, surveys for condition reports or insurance purposes.

Ivybridge Marine Ltd, Bottom Lock, Dark Lane, Braunston (01327 704847) are boat builders and Dutch barge specialists.

JG Marine Services, operate the large covered slipway at Bottom Lock, Dark Lane,

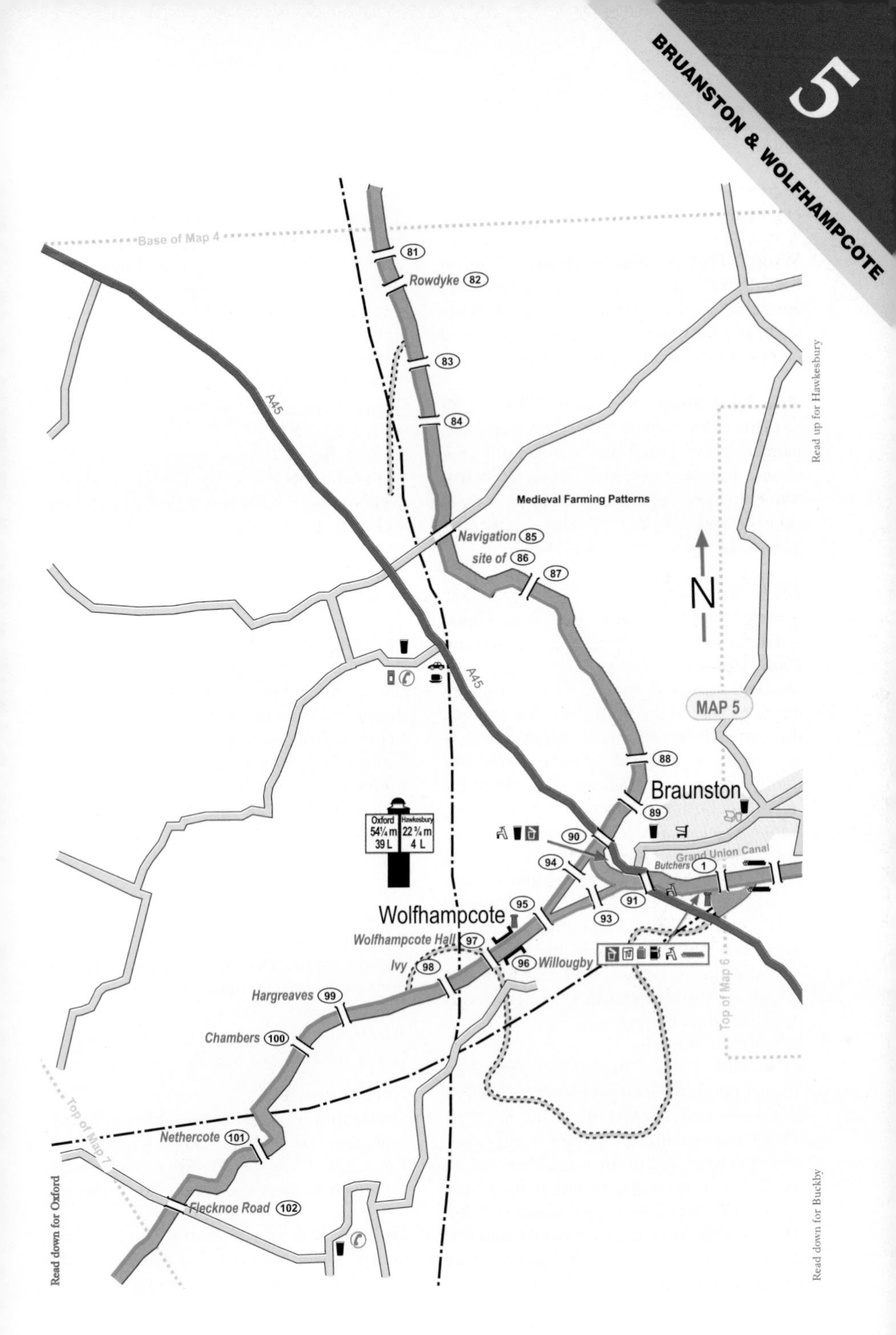
Base of Map 4
81
Rowdyke 82
83
84
A45
Medieval Farming Patterns
Navigation 85
site of 86
87
N
A45
MAP 5
88
Braunston
89
Oxford 54¼ m 39 L
Hawkesbury 22 ¾ m 4 L
90
94
Grand Union Canal
Butchers 1
91
93
Wolfhampcote
95
Wolfhampcote Hall 97
96 Willougby
Ivy 98
Hargreaves 99
Chambers 100
Top of Map 6
Top of Map 7
Nethercote 101
Flecknoe Road 102
Read up for Hawkesbury
Read down for Oxford
Read down for Buckby

Braunston (07071 226141). CORGI gas and engine fitting, repairs and callouts.

Wharf House Narrowboats, Bottom Lock, Dark Lane, Braunston (01788 899041) specialise in the internal systems of boats such as gas, water and heating. They also carry out repairs and fit out complete craft.

The Boat Shop, Bottom Lock (01788 891310). Provisions & groceries, souvenirs, painted ware, brassware, stitchcraft, deck shoes, rainwear, videos, books & maps. Summer opening: 8.00am–8.00pm 7 days, June to Sept. Winter opening 8.00am–6.00pm, 7 days, Oct–May.

Bridges 2–5

A flight of six locks raises the Grand Union Canal through 35ft to the three mile summit pound that ends at Buckby Top Lock. Beside the bottom lock is the old Grand Junction dry dock and facing it on the other side are three fine Georgian canal cottages. The cottage by the second lock actually stands over the by-weir, which made for easy plumbing in pre-pollution conscious days! The Admiral Nelson (Lock 3) is a popular boating pub dating back to 1730, serving Ruddles, Websters & Carlsberg and a range of traditional ales. It offers home cooked meals evenings and lunchtimes, 7 days a week. In hot weather patrons use the garden or the lockside terrace, and in winter the sound of Northamptonshire skittles reverberates around the bar.

Braunston Tunnel

2,048 yds. Unlike Blisworth, Braunston Tunnel posed few real problems to Jessop's engineers and opened on time in 1796. There was one minor blunder during construction when two of the contractors set off on different bearings, resulting in a kink about 400 yards from the eastern end. Though little more than curiosity today, this did pose problems for fully loaded 'pairs' which could not pass each other at this point for fear of getting wedged.

The two Grand Junction tunnels were a severe bottleneck when boats were horse-drawn and had to be 'legged' through, but the coming of steam tugs in 1871 helped matters considerably. The tugs survived until 1934, by which time most boats were motorised.

The horse path over the top of Braunston Tunnel makes an interesting walk.

Welton

A short distance from Bridge 6 stands Welton, where walkers will find a refreshing welcome at the White Horse, which has a restaurant. Meals and snacks are always available, skittles, garden . . . and mind the steps!

Bridges 6–10

The canal emerges from the tunnel cutting into pleasant open countryside with views across to Welton. Daventry feeder enters between Bridges 6 and 7. From Bridge 8 southbound boaters will catch their first glimpse of Norton Junction and the Leicester Line of the GU. The close-cropped turf of the pasture has a healthy appearance and dark-faced sheep speckle the verdant landscape.

Daventry

1 3/4 miles south. All services. Though of ancient origin, Daventry is today a rapidly growing industrial town. This aside, many old houses remain, including the Wheatsheaf Inn where Charles I stayed before the Battle of Naseby.

Norton Junction

Overlooked by an attractive little toll house, now used as holiday accomodation, the Leicester Line heads away northwards, eventually to meet the Trent near Derby.

See the *Waterways World Guide to the Grand Union (Leicester Section)* for the route northwards from Norton Junction.

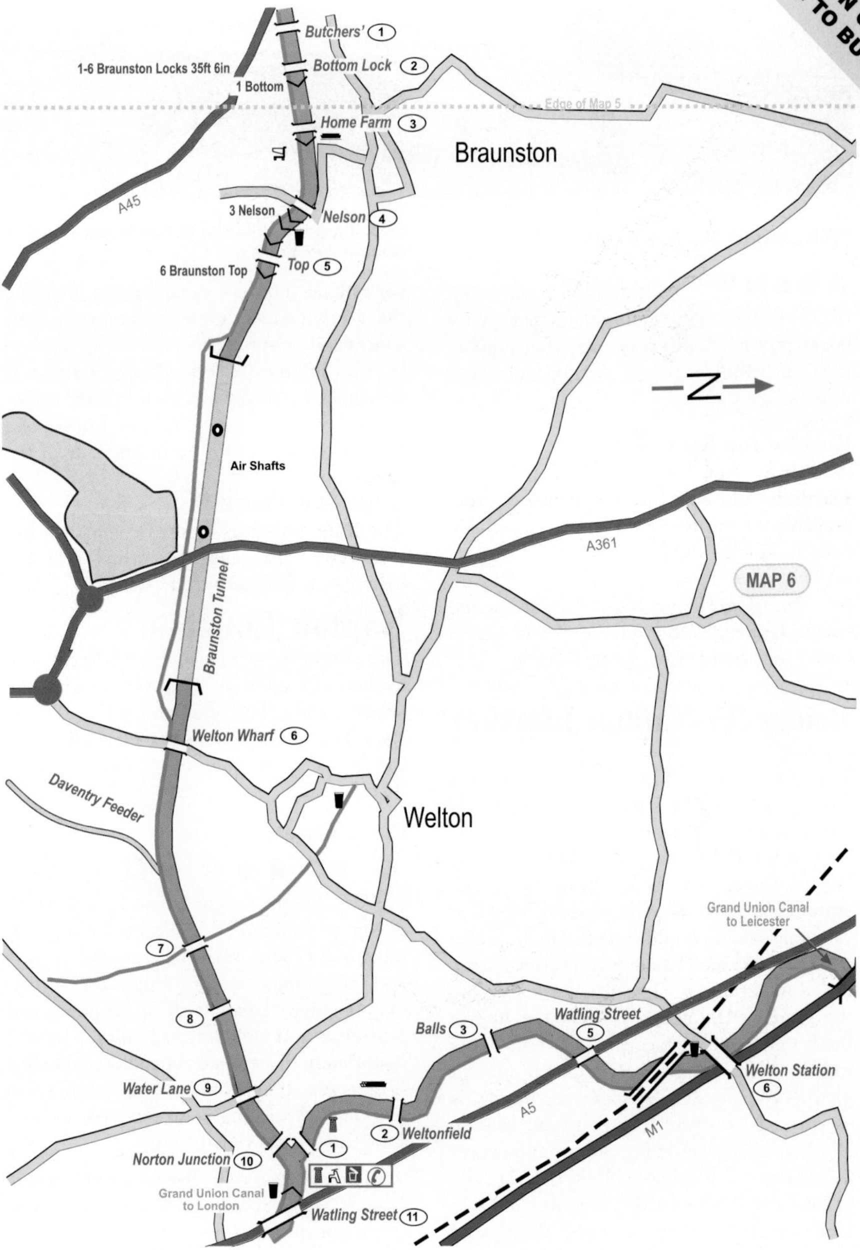

Read up for Braunston

MAP 6

Butchers' 1
Bottom Lock 2
1-6 Braunston Locks 35ft 6in
1 Bottom
Edge of Map 5
Home Farm 3
Braunston
A45
3 Nelson
Nelson 4
Top 5
6 Braunston Top
N
Air Shafts
A361
Braunston Tunnel
Welton Wharf 6
Daventry Feeder
Welton
Grand Union Canal to Leicester
7
8
Balls 3
Watling Street 5
Welton Station 6
Water Lane 9
2 Weltonfield
A5
M1
1
Norton Junction 10
Grand Union Canal to London
Watling Street 11

Heading north onto the Grand Union Canal at Napton Junction.

Weltonfield Narrowboats

Weltonfield, Daventry. (01327 842282, www.weltonfield.co.uk). Hire boats, pump out, gift shop, chandlery, moorings, boatbuilding and fitting and boat repairs.

Buckby Top Lock

The New Inn is a free house serving Marston's and Sam Smith's. Food is always available lunchtimes and evenings, canalside garden, skittles and payphone.

See the *Waterways World Guide to the Grand Union (North)* for the Grand Union Canal southwards from Long Buckby.

Bridge 95–Napton Junction

See map 5

The Oxford Canal joins with the Grand Union Canal over a 5-mile section of broad beam waterway, enlarged by the latter company in the 1930s, along the 1830 line of the Oxford Canal. The broad beam barge-like craft of 66 tons carrying capacity, which it was envisaged would revolutionise water transport between London and Birmingham, never materialised. The canal runs across the grain of the countryside at the foot of Bush (539ft) and Beacon (678ft) hills doing well to avoid lockage. It is a remote unpeopled landscape, little changed for hundreds of years. If you want company you have to climb up to the windy, but remote and peaceful, village of Flecknoe (T, PH). The Old Olive Bush opens in the evenings only. At Wolfhampcote a reedy pool disappears beneath an obvious canal bridge, marking the old roundabout route to Braunston. Only a farm and a church (restored a few years ago by the 'Friends of Friendless Churches'!) remain of a village swept away by field enclosures. Two abandoned railway lines cross each other adding to the melancholy of the scene.

Lower Shuckburgh

The little church is a gem of golden ochre coloured stone, and the pretty cottages belong to the Shuckburgh estate.

Napton Junction

The southern section of the Oxford Canal begins and ends at its junction with the Grand Union. The junction itself is a lonely spot. The Grand Union branches off under Bridge 17 en route to Warwick and Birmingham.

Calcutt Boats

(01926 813757). On the Grand Union $^1/_4$ mile north of Napton Junction. Hire craft (including day hire), solid fuels, mooring, craneage, repairs and servicing, boatbuilding and fitting, maintenance (particularly of engines and gearboxes and including call outs), painting, Boat Safety Inspections, chandlery and shop (groceries, books and gifts), slipway in marina. 70ft turning point for boats visiting from the Oxford Canal.

See the *Waterways World Guide to the Grand Union (North)* for the Grand Union Canal northwards from Napton.

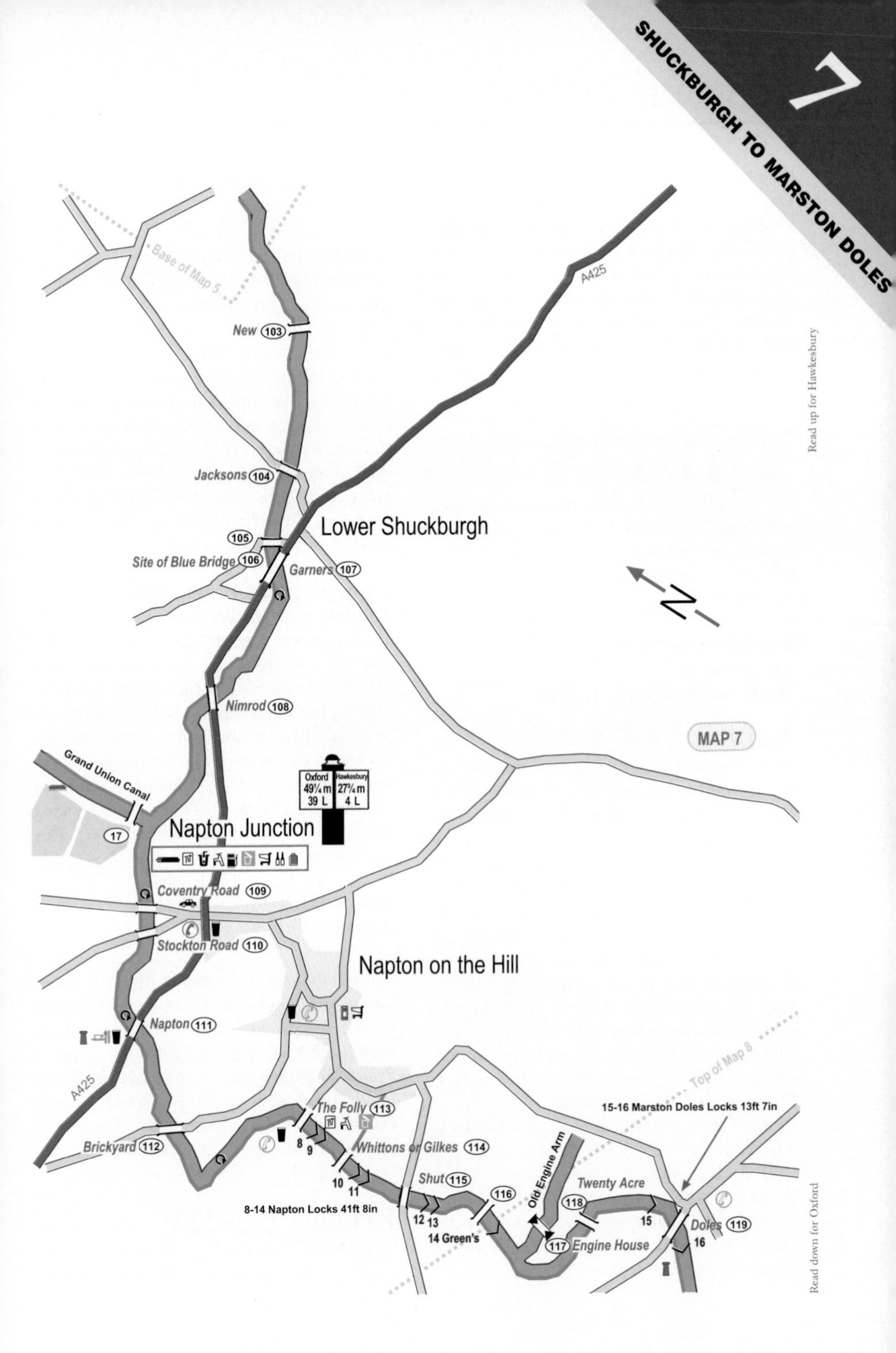

Read up for Hawkesbury

Read down for Oxford

The Napton Bridge Inn by Bridge 111 offers Davenports, traditional Sunday lunches. There is a canalside beer garden and children's play area and a winding hole outside for those not intending to continue up the locks. The King's Head, south of Bridge 109 is a free house serving Hook Norton ales, and restaurant and bar meals lunchtime and evening, except Sunday and Monday evenings.

Napton Narrowboats Ltd

(01926 813644). Hirecraft, pumpout, slipway, moorings, repairs and servicing (including breakdown callouts), boatbuilding and fitting, shop (souvenirs, chandlery, provisions) and off-licence.

Black Prince Holidays

(01527 575115). Hire craft.

Napton

This pleasant village clings to the hillside facing southwards and on a fine day offers glorious views over the attractive Warwickshire countryside, including the Napton flight of locks. The prominent windmill has been restored and has a fine set of new vanes, making it a famous landmark. The best access to the village is from Bridge 113 where there are moorings and it's about 10 minutes walk to the village centre where may be found the Crown and a post office/stores, complete with off licence and a bakery on the premises which is open every day but only in the morning on Sundays. Phone cards are also available.

At the bottom of the Napton flight of locks is The Folly (01962 815185), at one time the Bull & Butcher of *Narrow Boat* fame. Reopened after 44 years this free house offers meals, including a breakfast every day except Mondays. Children are welcome. It also has a public telephone. Adjacent is the Folly Canal shop with gifts and some chandlery.

A winding hole is situated between Bridges 112 and 113. Boaters not intending to navigate to Fenny Compton and beyond are asked to turn here, so conserving water. Boats approaching from the summit and wishing to turn soon are requested either to wind above Marston Doles top lock (if length allows) or in the entrance to the Engine Arm, and not to proceed all the way down the locks merely tor the sake of it. Please conserve water at all times as the Napton flight is often one of the first to be affected by water shortage restrictions in times of drought.

Napton Engine House Arm

This 900-yard long arm once led to a pumping engine which lifted water up into a brick channel running to the canal summit above Marston Doles. With the construction of Boddington Reservoir in 1811 the pump was considered redundant and went out of use. 1974 saw the resumption of regular backpumping during the summer months at Napton and Marston Doles Locks using modern equipment situated by the locks. The arm is now used for moorings.

Neil Adkins (01926) 812225). Moorings, caravan and camping site.

Those mooring at the top of Marston Doles Locks will find the nearest refreshment almost two miles away at the Holly Bush (01327 260934, www.hollybushinn.com) at Priors Marston where food is available every lunch time and evening (except Sunday evenings). As well as bed and Breakfast accomodation transport to and from the locks can be organised.

Bridges 127–135

The Oxford Canal's 11 mile summit must qualify as the classic example of the contour

Picture: Colin Underhill

The classic view of the Oxford Canal; from the windmill the Napton flight of locks alongside the village is clearly visible leading towards the canal's summit.

canal as it clings unyieldingly to the natural curves of the landscape. Nowhere can this be better appreciated than from Wormleighton Hill. The canal virtually encompasses this, so much so, that Bridge 127 is only 950 yards from the canal on the other side of the hill, and yet is separated from it by at least two miles of waterway. To get the full feel of these twists and turns keep an eye on Wormleighton radio mast and try to keep your feet in one position!

Fenny Compton

The village is over a mile from the wharf, and with most services within easier reach at other points along the canal there is little to draw the boater this far afield. The well known George & Dragon by Bridge 136 has become The Wharf Inn but still boasts a restaurant (01295 770332 for reservations).

Fenny Marina (01295 770461). Pumpout, solid fuel, slipway, moorings, brokerage. The shop sells a wide range of books, maps, guides, and there's a large chandlery.

Within the marina are **Fenny Boat Services** (01295 770934) who operate wet and dry docks and repair engines and boats, having an emphasis on boat fitting and the engineering systems involved.

Fenny Compton'Tunnel'.
In spite of having been 'opened out' for over 100 years, this section is still known as 'The Tunnel'. Originally 1,138 yards in length, the tunnel was an expensive bottleneck. In 1838 the company managed to buy the land over the tunnel and proceeded to open out parts of it at both ends and in the middle leaving the two detached portions discernable today. The going is very slow – you might only be able to make 2 mph before you create a wash.

Bridge 142 is the towpath bridge crossing the feeder from Boddington Reservoir 2½ miles to the east.

Claydon

Standing sentinel on its hilltop, Claydon is the most northerly of Oxfordshire villages, and has an out-on-a-limb feel to it. The tiny church is charming the clock strikes the hours but has no face. There used to be a Gilbertine Priory at the nearby hamlet of Clattercote but now only an arch, vault and gable bear witness to the lost history of what today is a farm. Claydon deserves to be visited for its Bygones Museum – a fascinating exhibition of curiosities from the agricultural and domestic life of days past and also includes a traction engine, steam roller and several model steam engines. Steam Days are the first Sunday of each month plus Bank Holiday Sundays and Mondays from April to September. An annual vintage fayre is held on the first Saturday and Sunday in August. There is a small admission charge and it's open daily (except Mondays but including Bank Holidays) from April to December. Parties by arrangement (01295 690258, bygonesmuseum@yahoo.com). There is a shop selling local crafts and gifts as well as a restaurant offering morning coffee, lunches and afternoon teas, with evening meals available by appointment – all home made using local seasonal produce.
Claydon House nearby is open for morning coffees and afternoon teas
The group of buildings at the top of the Claydon Flight of locks were formerly canal maintenance workshops but are now a source of local hand painted canalware and gifts.
There is no access at Bridge 144/Claydon Top Lock.

Cropredy

In recent times some modern development has rather marred Cropredy's overall attractiveness, but there is still much to be said for the peaceful charm of this typical Oxfordshire village, best known for the Civil War battle fought nearby in 1644, some relics

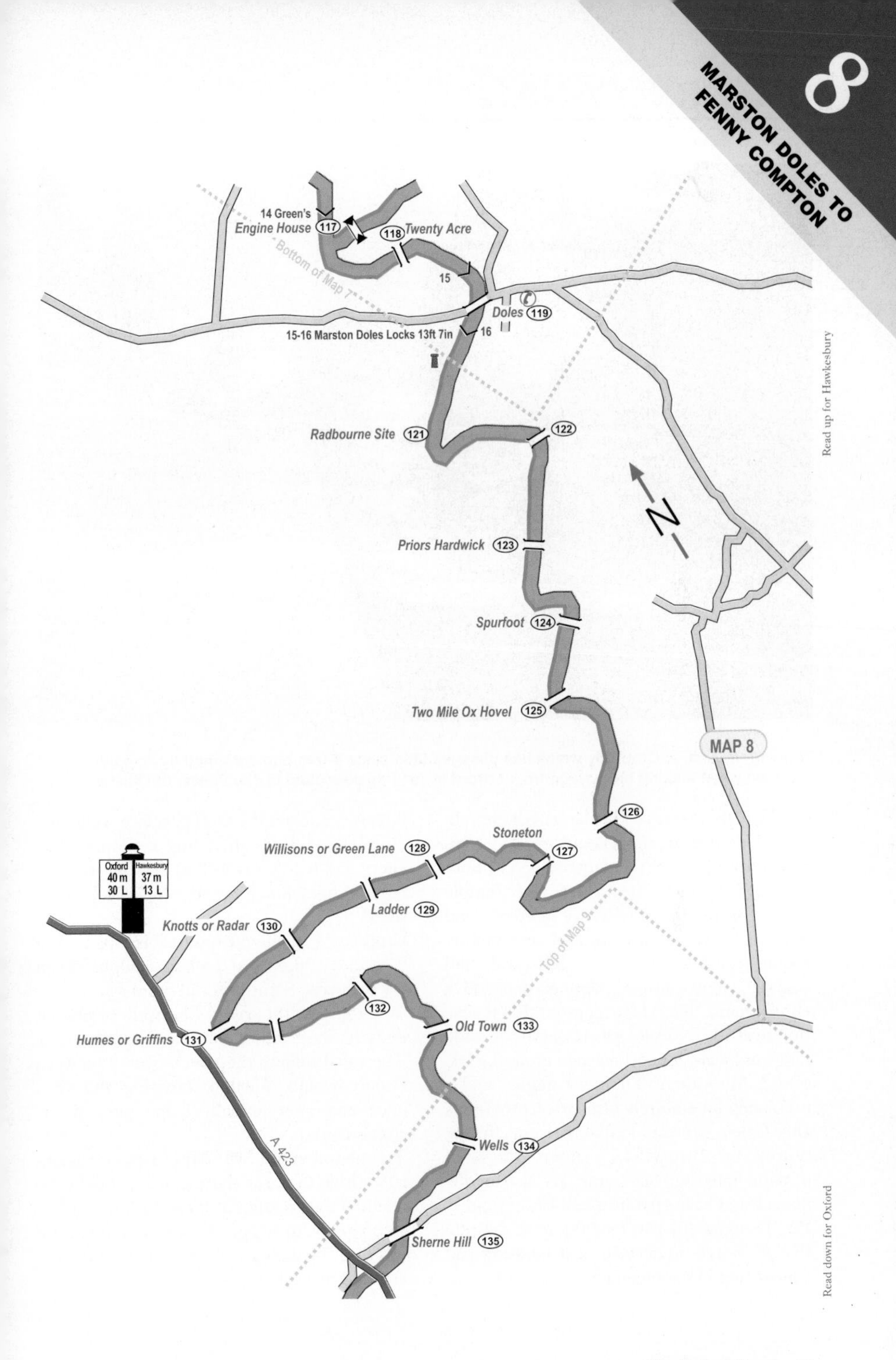

Read up for Hawkesbury

Read down for Oxford

Picture: Euan Corrie

Entering the lock at Cropredy which has changed little since it was photographed by Temple Thurston when making his voyage from Oxford in 1911 as described in The Flower of Gloster.

of which are preserved in the parish church. The Red Lion (appropriately, up Red Lion Street from the lock) was mentioned by both L.T.C. Rolt in *Narrow Boat*, and Temple Thurston in *The Flower of Gloster*, and remains largely unaltered, and very picturesque. It offers a variety of ales, meals and snacks. There's also a patio garden and a family room. The 17th century Brasenose Inn near the village green serves a wide range of meals, lunchtimes and evenings (ex. Sun & Mon eves). There's a garden and a tuck-shop for children. Groceries, provisions and Calor gas are available from Bridge Stores by Bridge 153, open Mon–Sat 6.30am–6pm, Sun 9am–5pm. It's also an off-licence and keeps paraffin and Elsan fluid.

Pan Designs (01295 758297) next door to Bridge Stores, undertake boat painting and signwriting by arrangement.

Green Scene, on the Green, sells a wide variety of local crafts including ceramics, jewellery and textiles as well as serving tea, coffee and light lunches and is open six days a week.

Cropredy's small post office is open from 9.30am–12.30pm and 2.30pm–5.30pm except on Tuesdays, Saturdays and Sundays.

At Cropredy the river Cherwell begins or ends its association with the Oxford Canal. The canal follows the river's course between Cropredy and Thrupp, crossing the river once and later actually using part of the river's course.

The pound above Slatt Mill Lock is particularly prone to water shortages, essentially the result of the greater fall at this lock (8ft) when compared with Cropredy Lock which feeds it (5ft 6in). Boaters are asked to take particular care not to waste water.

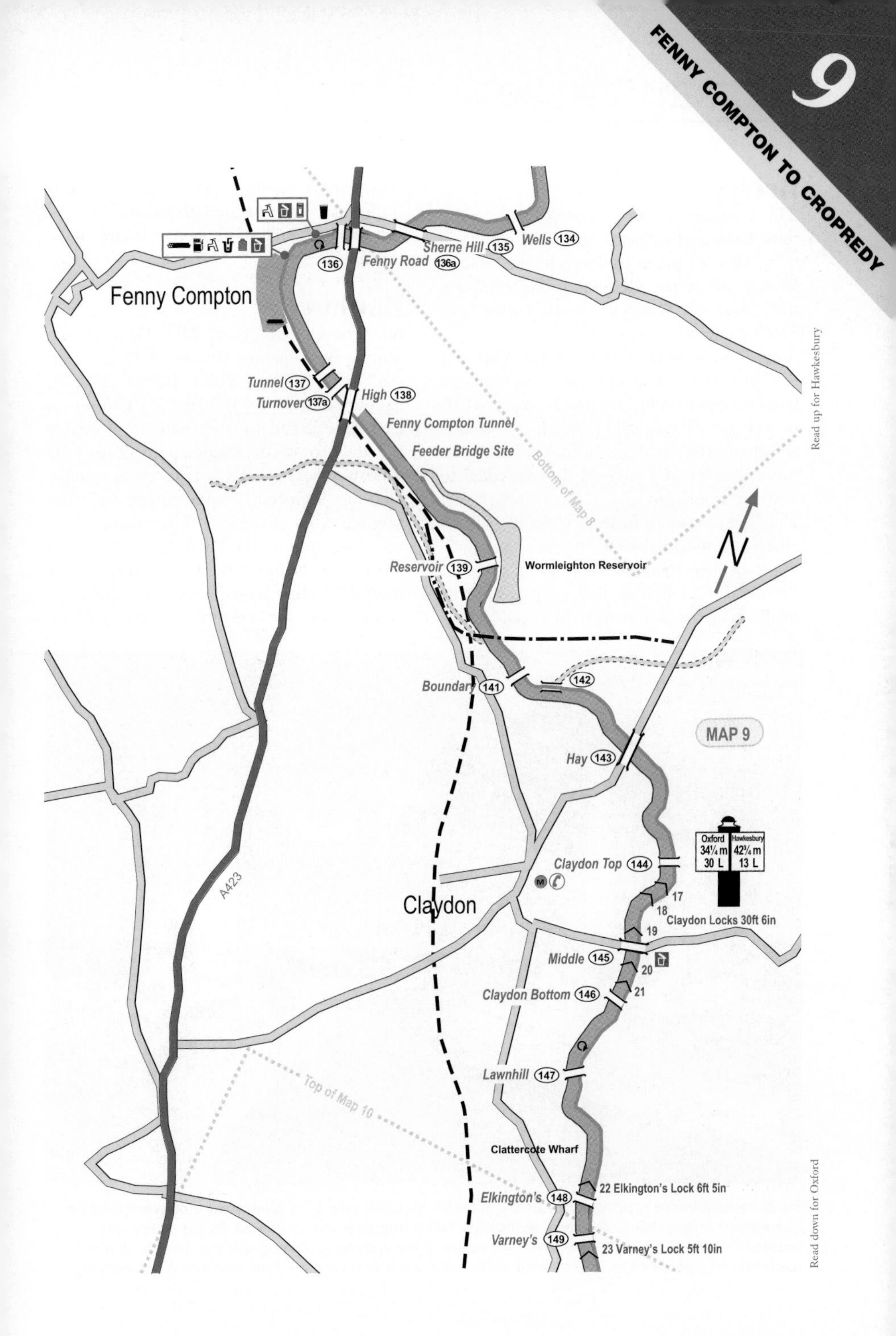
Fenny Compton
136
Fenny Road 136a
Sherne Hill 135
Wells 134
Tunnel 137
Turnover 137a
High 138
Fenny Compton Tunnel
Feeder Bridge Site
Bottom of Map 8
Reservoir 139
Wormleighton Reservoir
Boundary 141
142
MAP 9
Hay 143
Oxford 34¼ m 30 L
Hawkesbury 42¾ m 13 L
Claydon Top 144
17
18
Claydon Locks 30ft 6in
19
Claydon
A423
Middle 145
20
Claydon Bottom 146
21
Lawnhill 147
Top of Map 10
Clattercote Wharf
22 Elkington's Lock 6ft 5in
Elkington's 148
Varney's 149
23 Varney's Lock 5ft 10in
Read up for Hawkesbury
Read down for Oxford

Bridges 160–164

The northern outskirts of Banbury show the town to be a prosperous industrial conurbation. The tall green building to the west of Bridge 162 is the General Foods complex, the home of Maxwell House coffee and Bird's custard.

A new road joining the A423 to the A361 and the M40 extension crosses the canal opposite General Foods. The famous Grimsbury Lift Bridge has disappeared beneath the roundabout and the canal has been diverted, leaving a quarter of a mile of the old canal to serve as moorings.

The bend between Bridges 163 and 164 is a sharp one, please slow down when approaching, especially if coming from the north.

Factory Street Bridge had been incongruously reinstated amongst the redevelopments above Banbury Lock as an apparently traditional Oxford Canal lift bridge, but you will need a windlass to operate its hydraulic mechanism.

Banbury

All services, EC Tues, MD Thur & Sat. Tourist Information Centre, 8 Horse Fair, (01295 259855, Fax 01295 270556, banbury.tic@cherwell-dc.gov.uk) Banbury is a strong contender for any national award for the town most determoined to destroy its waterway heritage. Its famous cross is actually a Victorian replacement of the original cross of nursery rhyme fame which was destroyed by the Puritans in 1602. It is situated at the top of the High Street. A walk there will take you past most of Banbury's shops and the restored Market Place.

Banbury acquired a reputation for caring little for its canal when the basins were converted into a bus station in the 1960s. The local authority's latest improvement is this shopping centre and museum which completely overpower the scale of the waterway, consigning the historic drydock uselessly to a glass case, and leaving potential visitors to tie up in a concrete and glass canyon.

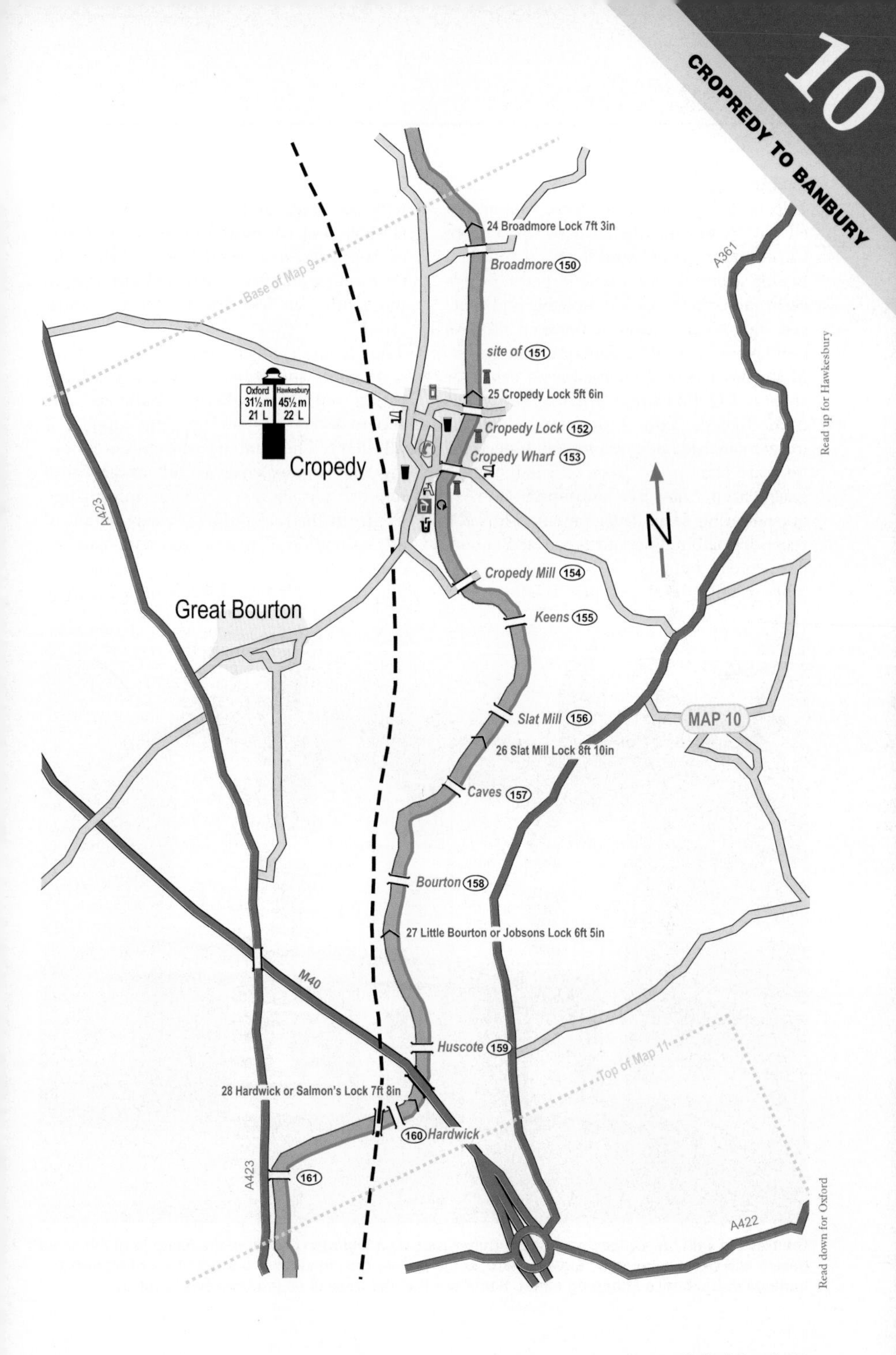

Read up for Hawkesbury

Read down for Oxford

Banbury also has what is probably the only cinema the Odeon in the Horse Fair, situated within walking distance of the Oxford Canal (other than Oxford itself). If you want to stop overnight it's a case of getting there early, and even then you'll probably find yourself moored in a canyon between modern buildings or beneath a concrete road bridge.

Much has changed on Banbury's canalside since L.T.C. Rolt wrote *Narrow Boat*. Apart from Tooley's Yard, little remains of the former canalside neighbourhood. Indeed the boatyard has now been turned into a glass-cased novelty swamped by an overpowering retail development. Thus 200 years of boatbuilding and repair at Banbury has come to an end.

The retail development, Castle Quay Shopping Centre, includes many major national names and can supply all types of clothing and consumer goods while Tesco, on Southam Road, immediately north of the town centre and Sainsburys, at Calthorpe, to the south, can feed the hungriest of boat crews.

The town is well served with many restaurants and public houses, if you fancy eating out, and bakeries, butchers and supermarkets to stock up your supplies if you don't. The Banbury Museum overlooking the famous cross is full of historical interest and there's a Tourist Information Centre at the same address where details of attractions and places to visit can be obtained.

The Spiceball Sports & Recreation Centre is

Picture: Euan Corrie

Contrasting with the replacement of Banbury Cross by a Victorian imitation, the filling in of the canal basins and overwhelming of Tooley's Yard, is the private preservation of a small piece of signwritten heritage in Banbury's shopping street. Some say that this view is all the town has to offer!

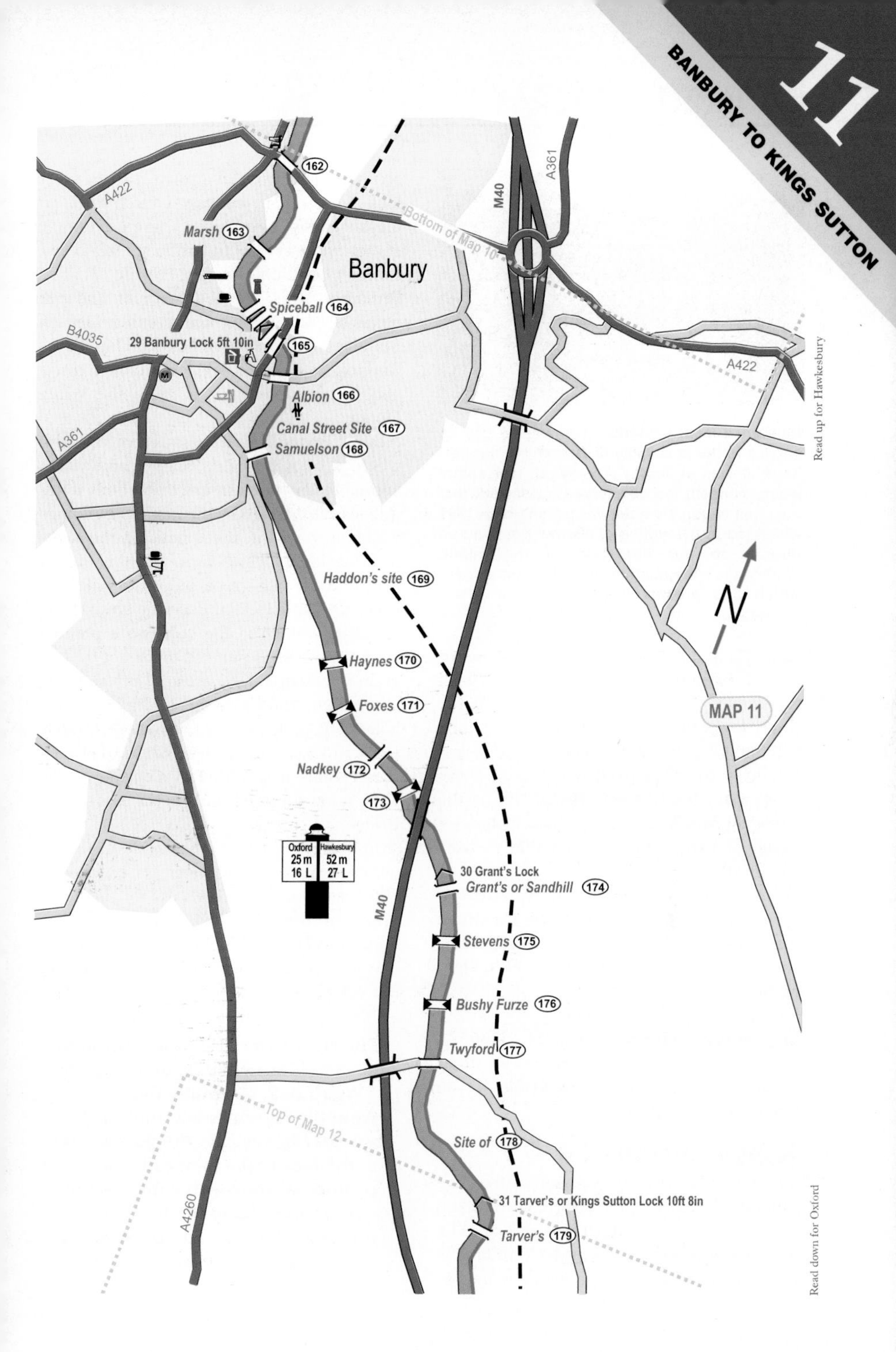

11
BANBURY TO KINGS SUTTON
A422
162
M40
A361
Bottom of Map 10
Marsh 163
Banbury
Spiceball 164
B4035
29 Banbury Lock 5ft 10in
165
A422
Albion 166
Canal Street Site 167
A361
Samuelson 168
Read up for Hawkesbury
Haddon's site 169
N
Haynes 170
Foxes 171
MAP 11
Nadkey 172
173
Oxford 25 m 16 L
Hawkesbury 52 m 27 L
30 Grant's Lock
Grant's or Sandhill 174
M40
Stevens 175
Bushy Furze 176
Twyford 177
Top of Map 12
Site of 178
31 Tarver's or Kings Sutton Lock 10ft 8in
A4260
Tarver's 179
Read down for Oxford

Picture: Euan Corrie

Banbury's local authority continues to pay lip service to the possibility of conserving our heritage. It was at Tooley's boatyard, lost somewhere beneath the developers' glasswork that Tom Rolt began his waterway adventure in 1939 which led to the writing of *Narrow Boat* and so directly to the formation of the Inland Waterways Association and the movement which has preserved many of our inland navigations.

near Banbury Lock and has an indoor heated swimming pool, open daily (from 6.45am to 10.00pm). Those who take the time to walk around to the far side will find a small plaque recording the height of 2000's river Cherwell floods, well above canal water level. Beside Bridge 165 is the Spiceball Mill Arts Centre which includes a snack bar and canalside beer garden (01295 257522).
Hurrans Garden Centre (01295 262041). Includes a tea room and restaurant which serves coffees teas and snacks between 9am and 3.30pm Mons–Sats and 10.30–4.30pm on Sundays.

Sovereign Marine (01295) 275657). Operate moorings with services for their occupants which may be available if you telephone in advance.

Kings Sutton

The village is effectively isolated from the canal by the un-bridged river Cherwell and the main Birmingham–Oxford railway. The only practical access involves a 1$^1/_2$ mile walk from Bridge 177. When you get there narrow streets radiate from an attractive green overlooked by a 15th century church with an elegant 198ft high spire. There's a railway station with services to Banbury, Oxford and London (see Public transport, page 13). The Butchers Arms serves restaurant and bar meals at lunchtimes and evenings except Mondays and Bank Holidays. The Three Tuns offers home cooked food at lunch times and evenings everyday, as does the White Horse.
Nearer Twyford Wharf stands Twyford Mill where Cherwell Valley Silos manufacture animal feeds. The original brick-built water mill stands dwarfed by the modern buildings which surround it, these housing the high-tech machinery which turns the likes of soya beans, straw and grape pulp into palatable bases for cattle fodder. Even the steam from the driers which is the only waste product from the works, is purified to extract the last grain of potential food material before being allowed into the atmosphere.
The M40 motorway crosses above Grant's Lock and again by Bridge 183, but between these points it is buried in a cutting to the west. A few hundred yards to the east of Nell Bridge is a garage.
Aynho Weir Lock is diamond-shaped to increase the volume of water passed through with each boat, to compensate for the depth (12ft) of the next lock down the canal, Somerton Deep. Shipton Weir Lock further down the canal is similarly constructed for the same reason.

The river Cherwell passes through the canal immediately above Aynho Weir Lock. Normally the 'draw' from the river's flow is only slight, but after heavy rain the flow across the face of the lock can cause problems. Approach with caution. In times of flood the headroom under Nell Bridge can prevent the passage of high-sided craft.

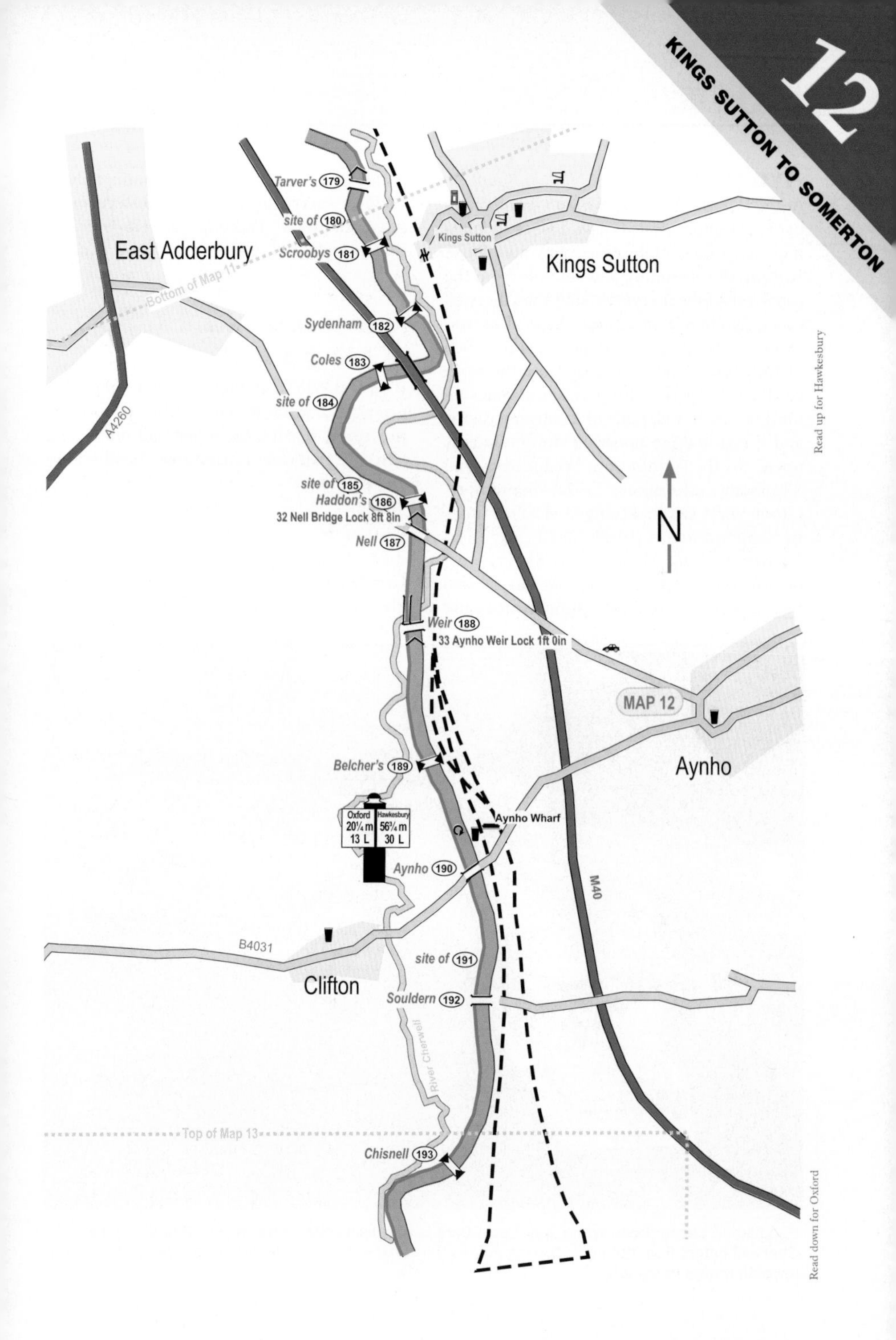
Tarver's 179
site of 180
Scroobys 181
East Adderbury
Bottom of Map 11
Kings Sutton
Kings Sutton
Sydenham 182
Coles 183
site of 184
A4260
site of 185
Haddon's 186
32 Nell Bridge Lock 8ft 8in
Nell 187
N
Weir 188
33 Aynho Weir Lock 1ft 0in
MAP 12
Aynho
Belcher's 189
Aynho Wharf
Oxford 20¼ m 13 L
Hawkesbury 56¾ m 30 L
Aynho 190
M40
B4031
site of 191
Clifton
Souldern 192
River Cherwell
Top of Map 13
Chisnell 193
Read up for Hawkesbury
Read down for Oxford

Aynho

At the Wharf, the Great Westem Arms offers bar snacks and meals 7 days a week in summer, a garden, children's room and Hook Norton Ales. Standing about a mile from the canal, on a hillside overlooking the Cherwell valley, Aynho is a charming village of narrow lanes, thatched cottages and rich Oxfordshire stone once away from the main road. Aynho park, with a classical mansion built on the foundations of a Norman castle, and a restored ice house in the grounds is open to the public on Wednesday and Thursday afternoons May–September. Group visits can be arranged at other times by appointment (01896 810636). The Cartwright Arms Hotel (01869 811111) just off the village green serves bar snacks and has a restaurant open lunchtimes and evenings every day. Two impressive railway viaducts carry the old Great Western main lines between Paddington, via Princes Risborough and Oxford, and the North-West.

Aynho Dock Services

(01869 338483). Pumpout, canal shop with groceries, gifts & souvenirs, chandlery, moorings, repairs, including call outs, Boat Safety Certificate inspections, boatbuildng and painting.

Clifton

The 17th century thatched Duke of Cumberland's Head serves a range of real ales, meals in the bar lunchtimes and

Picture: Euan Corrie

Heading up stream from Aynho Weir Lock. Care is necessary here after wet weather since the river Cherwell enters from the right, flowing across the canal to leave again over a weir beyond the long towpath bridge to the left.

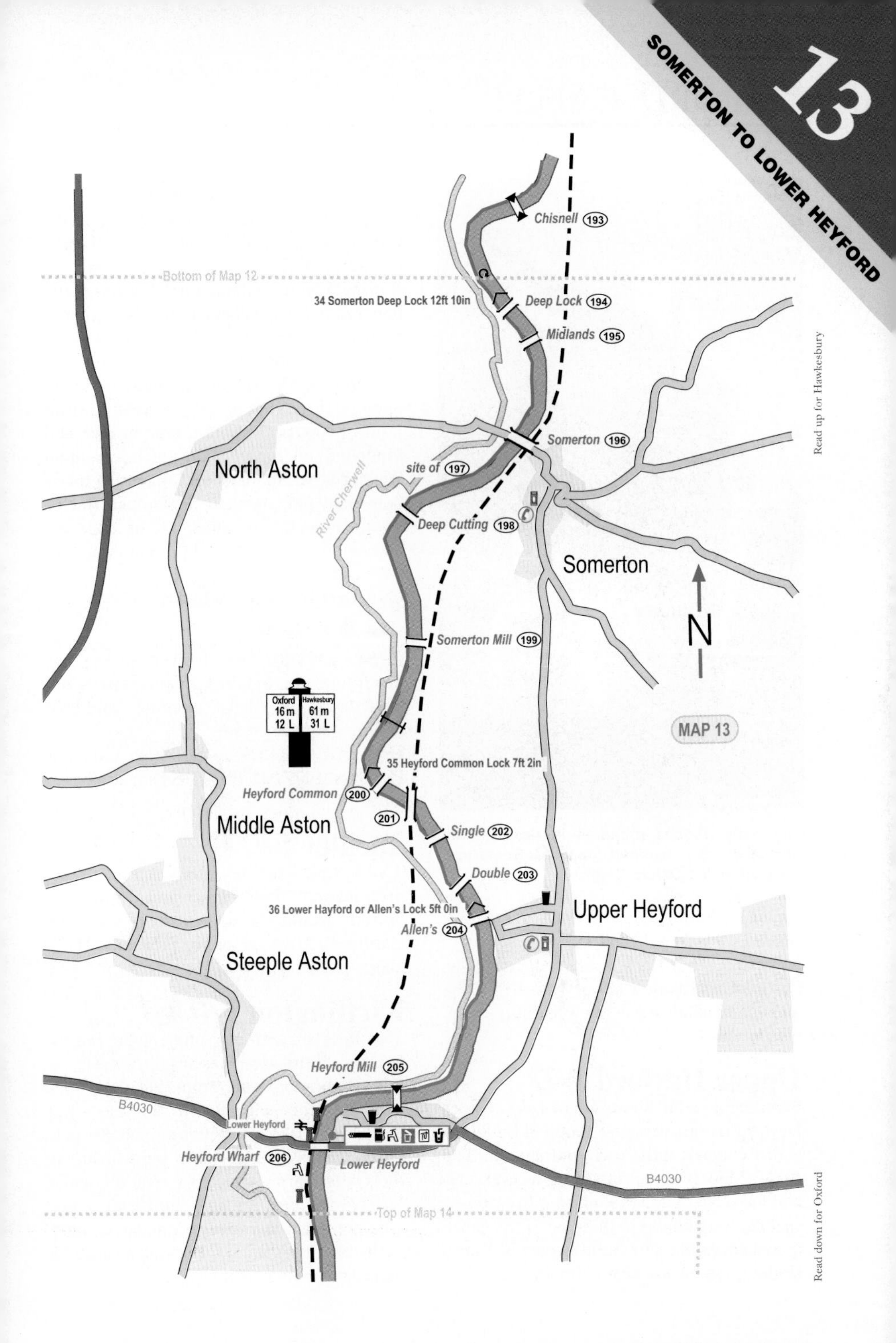

Read up for Hawkesbury
Read down for Oxford

Picture: Euan Corrie

The butty *Phoebe* prepares to descend the attractive and isolated lock at Somerton, deepest on the Oxford Canal.

evenings, and has a French restaurant (closed Mon eve) (01869 38534).
Somerton Deep Lock is the deepest on the Oxford Canal with a fall of 12ft. Below the lock the canal traverses pleasant, open, meadowland.

Upper Heyford

Standing on a hill above Allens Lock, Upper Heyford has an attractive group of buildings with its manor, tithe barn and church. The Barley Mow (Fullers) offers meals every day and has a beer garden. Rousham Eyecatcher, visible on its hilltop to the west of the canal, is a sham castle gate built as part of Kent's landscaping for Rousham House.

Lower Heyford

Sleepy village of yellow stone, with its 14th century church. The Bell serves draught cider and meals.
Rousham House (about a mile's walk) is the only example of William Kent's landscaping to have survived unaltered. The classical buildings, ponds, cascades, statues and vistas tantalise the visitor, the gardens being open throughout the year from 10am–4.00pm. The house, built in 1635 and modelled on early Tudor style, is open Wednesdays, Sundays and Bank Holidays 2pm–4.30 pm, April to September (inclusive). No children under 15, or dogs are allowed. It is unspoilt by commercialism such as tea room or shop.

Oxfordshire Narrowboats

(01869 340348). Hire craft including day hire, pump out, wet dock, engine repairs and breakdowns, boat hoist, moorings, and boat fitting, shop, ice cream.
Hire Boats from the Anglo Welsh Waterway Holidays (0117 927 7017) fleet are also based here.

Tackley

The footpath to the village makes a most pleasant walk. Pub, manor and Church are dotted around a spacious green. The Gardiner's Arms serves bar meals and Hall's beer.

Kirtlington

The Rock of Gibraltar offers John Smiths and Bass beers as well as snacks.
An invigorating walk from Pigeon's Lock leads to the village. To the east lies Kirtlington Park, well known for its polo ground. There is a choice of pubs including the Oxford Arms which has real ale and a variety of food available lunchtimes and evenings every day except Monday evening, in the bar or restaurant. Booking advised for Saturday evenings (01869 350208).

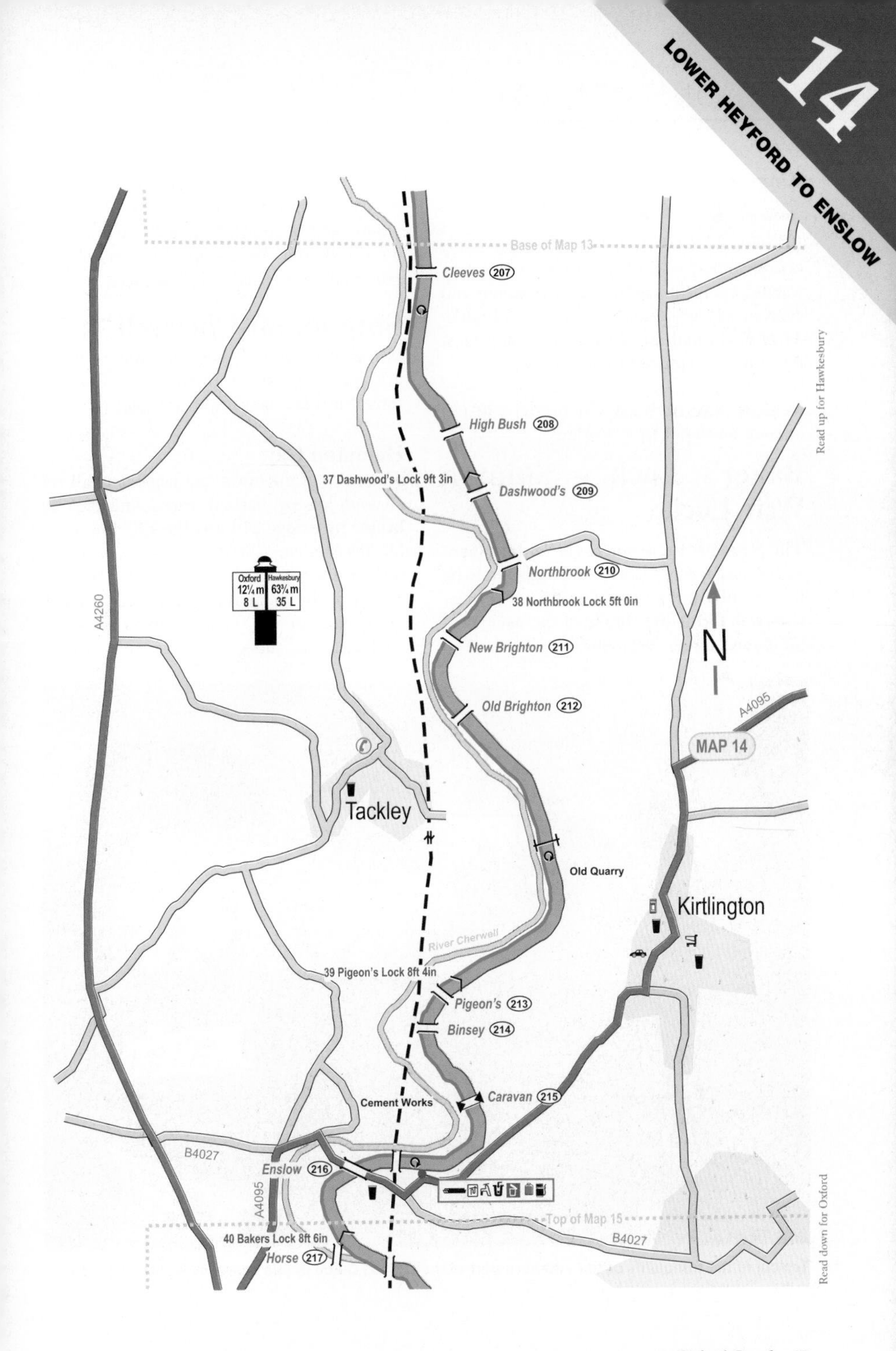
Base of Map 13
Cleeves 207
High Bush 208
37 Dashwood's Lock 9ft 3in
Dashwood's 209
Northbrook 210
38 Northbrook Lock 5ft 0in
New Brighton 211
Old Brighton 212
Oxford 12¼ m 8 L
Hawkesbury 63¾ m 35 L
A4260
A4095
MAP 14
N
Tackley
Old Quarry
Kirtlington
River Cherwell
39 Pigeon's Lock 8ft 4in
Pigeon's 213
Binsey 214
Cement Works
Caravan 215
B4027
Enslow 216
A4095
Top of Map 15
B4027
40 Bakers Lock 8ft 6in
Horse 217
Read up for Hawkesbury
Read down for Oxford

Kingsground Narrowboats

(01869 23344, www.kingsground.co.uk) operate moorings with pumpout, with a slipway for trailboats as well as a camping and caravan site close to the Rock of Gibraltar. They also build and fit out narrowboats at their unit on Heyford Business Park.

Avalon Narrowboat Co (01285 750567) operate hire craft from Enslow.

Baker's Lock – Shipton Weir Lock

The prominent remains of the large cement works near Baker's Lock were expected to be redeveloped at the time of writing. The river Cherwell forms the course of the navigation for almost a mile. Normally this river section constitutes no problem except for its sharp bends, but in times of flood it can be hazardous and boatyards may insist that hirers do not attempt the passage. Skippers of private craft are advised to do likewise.

Shipton-on-Cherwell

Garage with shop. Recording Studios, modern housing, and a picturesque Church, rebuilt in 1831, make up this village.

Hampton Gay

The ruins of the burnt-out Jacobean hall are surrounded by barbed wire. The railway bridge by Bridge 219 was the site of a terrible disaster on Christmas Eve 1874, when nine camages crashed over into the icy waters of the canal and 34 lives were lost. A gravestone in the churchyard remains to commemorate them.

Picture: Robin Smithett

Typical of the tranquility of the southern part of the Oxford Canal is this scene at Shipton Church.

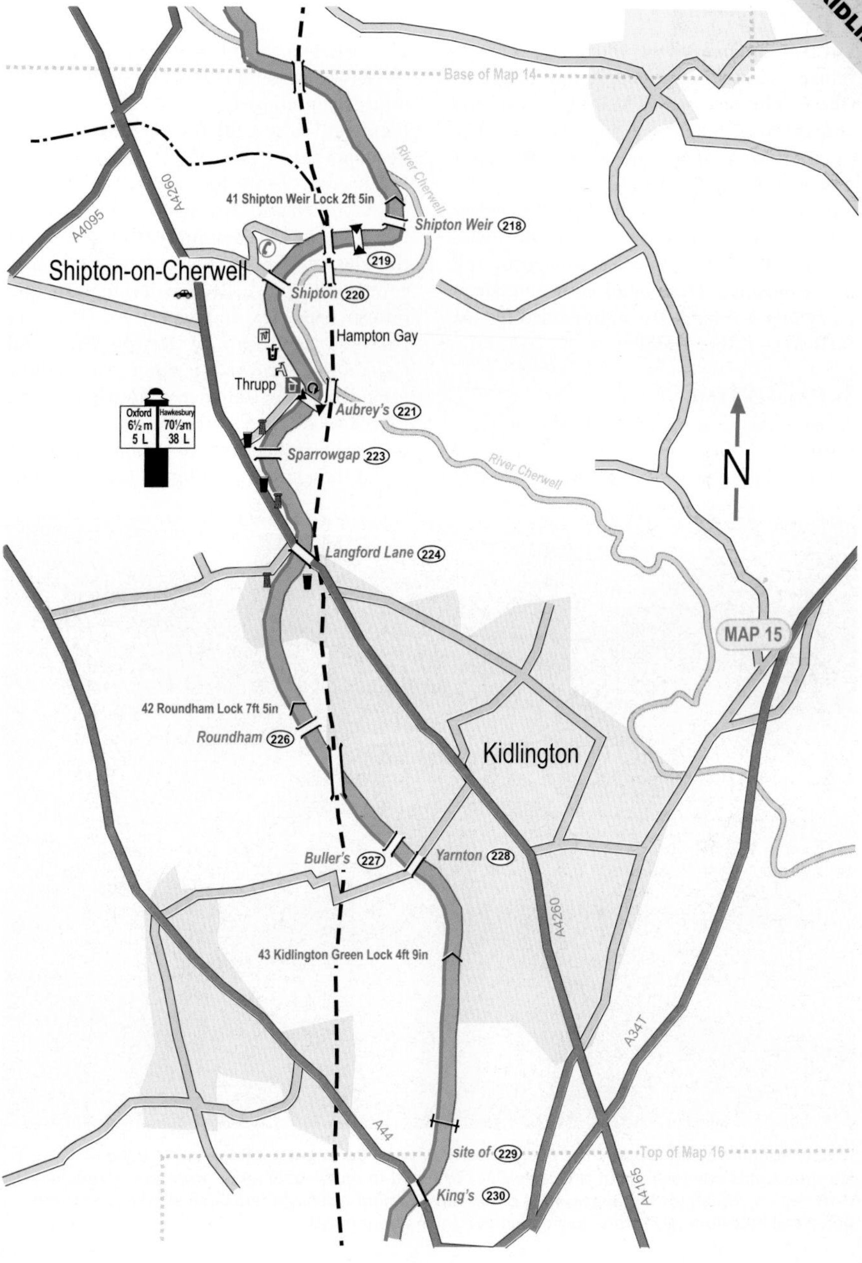

Base of Map 14
River Cherwell
41 Shipton Weir Lock 2ft 5in
Shipton Weir 218
219
A4260
A4095
Shipton-on-Cherwell
Shipton 220
Hampton Gay
Thrupp
Aubrey's 221
Oxford 6½ m 5 L
Hawkesbury 70½m 38 L
Sparrowgap 223
River Cherwell
N
Langford Lane 224
MAP 15
42 Roundham Lock 7ft 5in
Roundham 226
Kidlington
Buller's 227
Yarnton 228
A4260
43 Kidlington Green Lock 4ft 9in
A34T
A44
site of 229
Top of Map 16
King's 230
A4165

Read up for Hawkesbury

Read down for Oxford

Thrupp

Virtually unchanged in 100 years, Thrupp remains an almost perfect example of a canal village. The Boat serves Morrells, meals and snacks every lunchtime and evening. The canal's course joins (or leaves) the river Cherwell above Thrupp.

The Jolly Boatman, by Bridge 223, serves Morrells and guest beers, together with morning coffee and meals at lunchtime and in the evening. There is often live music at weekends. Booking is recommended for the restaurant (01865 377800).

Kidlington

All services. The canal skirts this modern town. The Wise Alderman by Bridge 224 serves Halls beer and meals every day. Restaurant booking is recommended (01865 377800). The canal between Bridge 224 and the left-hand bend is lined on both sides by industrial premises.

Blenheim Palace (01993 811325). A World heritage Site. $2^1/_2$ miles north-west of Kidlington. Built for the first Duke of Marlborough after his victory at the battle of Blenheim in 1704 and presently the home of the eleventh Duke. The impressive house, containing a fine collection of sculpture, furniture, paintings and tapestries stands in parkland laid out by Henry Wise and Capability Brown. Further attractions include the Italianate Gardens, the Marlborough Maze, rowing boats for hire on the lake, restaurant, gift shop, adventure playground and an exhibition to honour one

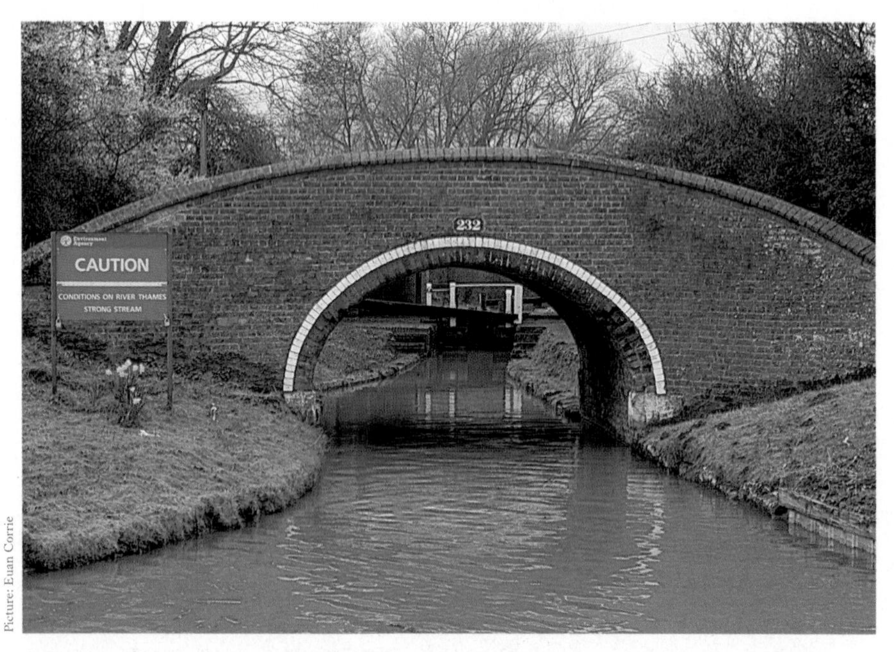

Picture: Euan Corrie

A view from the canal towards the river Thames, beyond the towpath bridge in the Duke of Marlborough's connecting cut is Duke's Cut Lock built to pass boats up or down to the variable river waters. Watch for the appearance of the Environment Agency's red signs warning of strong flows and therefore hazardous navigation conditions on the river.

of the Palace's most famous and respected sons, Sir Winston Churchill. The house is open daily 10.30am–4.45pm, mid March–end October and the park between 9am and 4.45pm all year.

NB. Bridge 228 is deceptively low.

The Duke's Cut

affords a short cut through to the Thames (see page 56). Using it boaters can bypass the canal through Oxford, but will need to purchase a licence at the first lock. The cut itself was dug at the request of the Fourth Duke of Marlborough to serve Wolvercote paper mill. At the time flood control on the Upper Thames was inadequate and the single stop-lock on the Cut required two sets of gates to cope with fluctuations in river level. Today only the abutments of this second pair can be seen, though the peculiar ground-paddle arrangement has been retained.

Picture: Euan Corrie

Watch out for the survivors of the once common Lock Distance Post on the southern part of the canal. They were once placed several hundred yards above and below most locks. The first boat past the post had the right to use the lock before craft approaching from beyond the lock – a rule intended to save violent disputes in the days when time was money to working boatmen.

Wolvercote

Separated by the canal and railway, the two halves of Wolvercote make a convenient stop for the boater. A mixture of very old and very new. Old Wolvercote stands on the edge of Port Meadow, near the Thames. Close to the mill (once supplied with coal by narrowboats which backed down the millstream to its wharf) are the White Hart and the Red Lion, both offering food. Handier for the canal, the Plough Inn by Bridge 236 serves bar snacks, has pub games, and a restaurant.
Bridge 239A gives access to a factory and is normally closed to boats. This lift bridge is electrically operated, and the lowering/raising button is to be found on the wall of the hut beside it.

College Cruisers

(01865 554343, www.collegecruisers.com). Hire craft, including day hire, pumpout, servicing and breakdowns.

Castlemill Boatyard

(01865 310930) (next door to College Cruisers) accomodates a hive of activities run as separate businesses providing moorings, chandlery, craneage, boatbuilding and repairs, engine repairs including breakdown call outs, boatfitting and even RYA Helmsmans Courses.

Rosamund The Fair is a restaurant boat based at Castlemill Boatyard and operating on both the river Thames and the canal. Advance booking is required for both individuals and groups (01865 55370, www.rosamundthefair.co.uk).

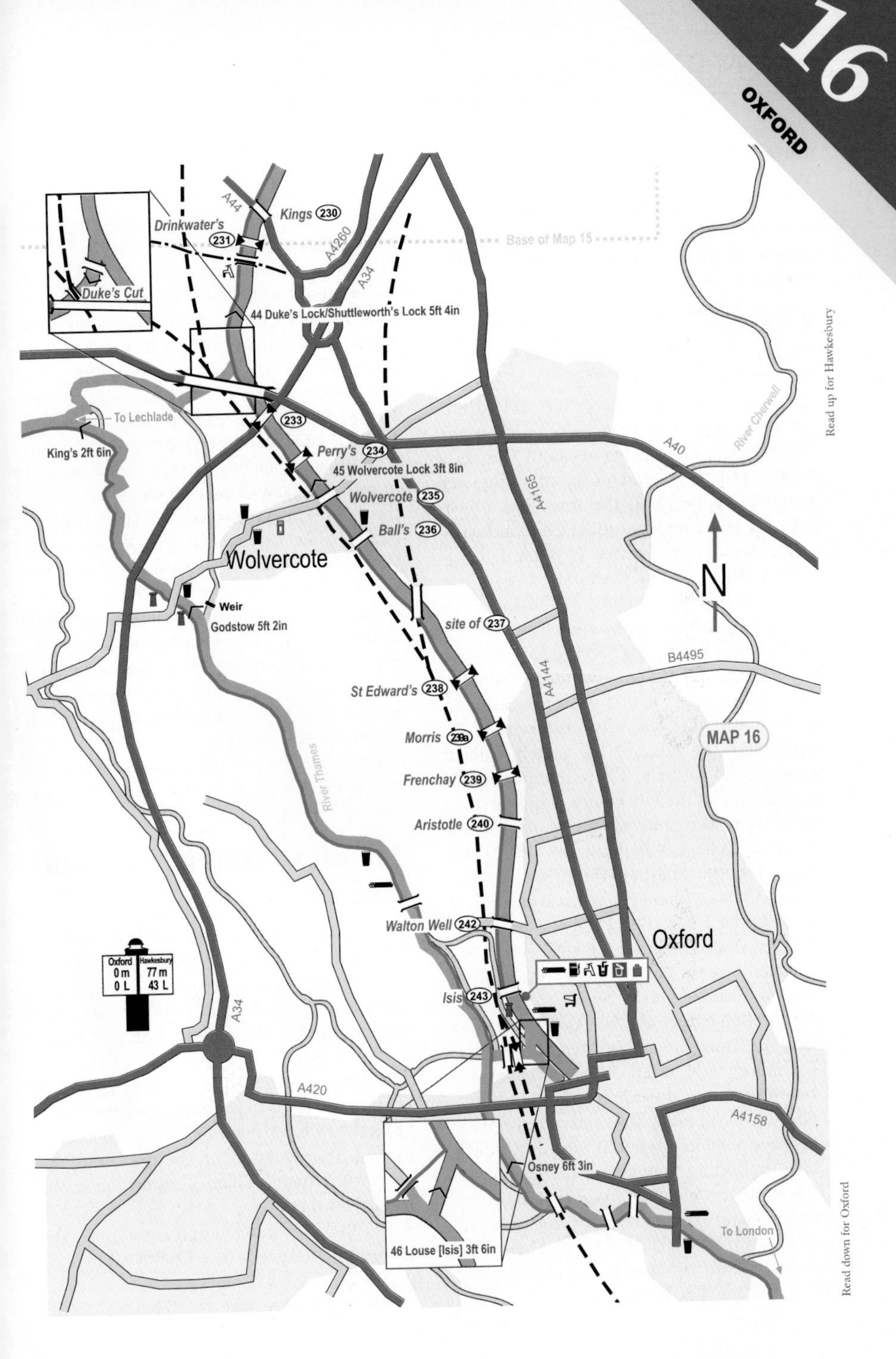
16
OXFORD
Base of Map 15
Read up for Hawkesbury
Read down for Oxford
A44
Kings 230
Drinkwater's 231
A4260
A34
Duke's Cut
44 Duke's Lock/Shuttleworth's Lock 5ft 4in
To Lechlade
King's 2ft 6in
233
Perry's 234
45 Wolvercote Lock 3ft 8in
Wolvercote 235
Ball's 236
Wolvercote
Weir
Godstow 5ft 2in
site of 237
A40
River Cherwell
A4165
N
B4495
A4144
St Edward's 238
Morris 239a
Frenchay 239
MAP 16
River Thames
Aristotle 240
Walton Well 242
Oxford
Isis 243
Oxford 0 m 0 L
Hawkesbury 77 m 43 L
A34
A420
A4158
Osney 6ft 3in
To London
46 Louse [Isis] 3ft 6in

Sheepwash Channel

A connection to the river Thames via Louse (or Isis) Lock. NB. In order to 'wind' at Oxford, boats over 50ft must lock through Louse Lock and wind below it in the Sheepwash Channel.

Oxford

All services. EC Thurs, MD Wed. Tourist Information Centre, The Old School, Gloucester Green, Oxford OX1 2DA (01865 726871). Oxford is first mentioned in the Anglo-Saxon Chronicles of about 912, as a walled settlement sited on an important river crossing. Since then, the town has grown into one of the major academic and industrial centres of the country. It is hard to say exactly when Oxford University began, but there were certainly scholars studying there in the 12th century. The first true colleges were founded soon after and today there are almost forty of them. Twentieth century development and the motor car have also left their mark, but the city still retains an atmosphere of calm in the stately college grounds and gardens. There is much to see in Oxford, and the city centre is only a short walk from the end of the canal. Since Nuffield College was built on the canal's original terminal basin in the 1930s the canal at Oxford has ended in an aquatic cul-de-sac below Louse Lock. There are now proposals to re-excavate the part of the basin now occupied by a car park. The Carfax Tower at the crossroads of Queen Street, Cornmarket Street, High Street and St. Aldates, is open every day, from the end of March to the end of October and offers superb views over Oxford's famous 'dreaming spires' skyline.

Oxford is particularly well blessed with pubs and keen explorers should have little difficulty in finding something to their taste. There are also plenty of places to eat, with a very wide and exciting range of cuisines. The city is an excellent place to shop. There's the market, and if you're a bookworm, Blackwell's in The Broad.

Theatres include The Apollo in George Street (01865 244544); the Playhouse, in Beaumont Street (01865 247134) and the Sheldonian in Broad Street (01865 277299).

Oxford has some impressive and famous museums: The Oxford Story, Broad Street, is a fantastic exhibition with many life-size dioramas, centred on the history and importance of Oxford and its University. The Ashmolean Museum in Beaumont Street lays emphasis on Ancient Egyptian and Eastern cultures. The Bodleian Library in The Broad is one of the six libraries entitled to receive a copy of every book published in the UK. Christ Church Picture Gallery boasts some exceptional Old Masters and Renaissance works. The Museum of Modern Art, Pembroke Street, concentrates on 20th century art forms with complementary films in the evening. The Museum of History & Science in The Broad has a fascinating collection of early scientific instruments. The Museum of Oxford, St Aldates, offers a good introduction to the city.

Contact the Tourist Information Office for details of guided walking or open top bus tours of the city.

Thames Detour around Oxford

As an alternative to retracing their course northwards back up the canal from Oxford, boaters can make a brief journey onto the Thames passing through two river locks and returning to the Oxford Canal via the Duke's Cut. At a cost.

The Thames is not administered by BW and boaters will need to pay a fee at either Osney or Godstow Lock if joining at Isis Lock, or if joining from Duke's Cut, the first Lock up, or down, stream. Thames visitors' licences last for six days.

For further information contact the Environment Agency (see Useful Addresses, page 12).

Those wishing to take the Thames detour

can lock through Isis or Louse Lock and turn sharp right across Castle Mill Stream to enter the Sheepwash Channel.
Having negotiated the railway bridge and passing through the river towpath bridge, you reach Fourstreams and the Thames proper. To the left is downstream, Osney Lock and Oxford, the route to the Kennet & Avon at Reading or Grand Union at Brentford. To the right is upstream and the way to Lechlade and the Duke's Cut.

Upstream to Duke's Cut

From Fourstreams the Thames is not particularly attractive until reaching Medley Weir, where, after passing under the footbridge by the old ferry cottage, Port Meadow spreads away to the right. Mooring against this extensive area of green pasture is unfortunately difficult as the banks are very shallow. As you proceed upstream, glance astern and see the spires of Oxford retreating behind you. Mooring is difficult except for the landing stage provided for customers of the Perch Inn at Binsey. Fifty yards from the river, this is a large historic 17th century thatched pub. Above Binsey the river widens, and the first of the two locks to be encountered on this short stretch of the Thames is Godstow Lock, situated on the left-hand bank of the river. Unlike locks on the Oxford Canal, but like all locks on the Thames, Godstow is manned by a resident keeper who will work the lock for you. Purchase your visitor's licence here if you don't already have one. Again, unlike the canal, the locks on the Thames are wide and it will be necessary to use mooring ropes when passing through them. Above the lock are the remains of Godstow Nunnery, built in 1138 and destroyed by the Roundheads in 1646. Here also is the historic and popular Trout Inn, and there are moorings between the low Godstow Bridge, and the high by-pass bridge on the left-hand bank for those wishing to patronise it. Food is available all day everyday in the low beamed interior or outside at tables overlooking the river.
Upstream, mooring places abound on the twisting reach (the river's equivalent of a 'Pound') to King's Lock. King's Lock is also attended by a resident keeper, but unlike locks downstream of it, is manually operated and the keeper will probably be glad of your assistance.
Above the lock the Thames is navigable to Lechlade (there are moves to make it so to Cricklade) and canal boaters may wish to explore upstream to Eynsham Lock, but to return to the Oxford Canal the boater must turn right above the lock into a labyrinth of backwaters, which gives access to the Duke's Cut. After entering the King's weirstream the boater must then turn sharp left into Wolvercote Mill Stream. This swings right followed by the A40 road and on the left, partly obscured by undergrowth, is the entrance to the Duke's Cut. The Cut was built by the order of the Duke of Marlborough and first connected the canal and the river in 1789 – a year before the canal reached Oxford itself. It was the only junction with the river until 1806, when the canal company built a wide lock at Isis to enable Thames river barges to reach the city. When it is recalled that until the completion of the Grand Junction Canal, the Oxford Canal and the Thames were the main waterway routes between the Midlands and London, it is interesting to contemplate that these narrow, twisting channels must have once carried a large number of boats and a considerable volume of traffic.

Today the Duke's Cut is a shallow and narrow channel about 400 yards long, which disappears under a narrow bridge carrying the railway and where the shallow Duke's Lock lowers the boats down the difference in level between river and canal.
The paddle gear on the bottom gates is conventional but the single ground paddle at the top gate has to be investigated through the small hole in the casing to ascertain its position. Having negotiated the lock and passed

under the towpath bridge you will find yourself back once again on the narrow waters of the Oxford Canal below Shuttleworth's Lock, having completed an interesting detour on the contrasting waters of the Thames.

Downstream to Oxford

Going downstream to Oxford the first hazard is Osney Bridge, the lowest on the river, which has the beneficial effect of preventing large boats passing into the upper reaches of the Thames. It should not present any problems to canal craft. To the right is East Street with its row of delightful houses ending with the Waterman's Arms. The Waterman's offers Greene King and Morland Ales with food, including home made pies, served at lunchtimes and evenings (except Sunday evenings). Booking is adviseable for Sunday lunch (01865 248832).

Canal boaters should be aware of the weirs which will drag the unsuspecting off course, and use the lay-by where boats can wait for the lock. These locks are mechanised and operated by a lock-keeper. When traffic is heavy the keeper will not only direct you to the required side of the lock, he will also dictate the order in which craft are to enter the lock. The use of ropes to control the boat as water enters or leaves the chamber is mandatory; engines must be stopped and radios etc., switched off. To the right of Osney Lock is the wharf occupied by the Environment Agency engineering department with its own large heated dry-dock. The white building adjacent to the lock is the District Navigation Office.

With Osney Lock behind you, the river continues between abandoned land once occupied by gas works and railway sidings. The obsolete railway bridge at George Island has now been converted to pedestrian use and treated to a gaudy paint scheme. After the footbridges comes a deft piece of steering as you swing across the current to pass between two wooden piles marking the safe channel through an ancient weir. Should you miss the turn, a little-used channel to the right will serve just as well, rejoining the main river below Folly Bridge, where the Thames is transformed once more into a river of beauty.

To the right are good free moorings (if possible always turn upstream to moor on any river); to the left the college boathouses line Christ Church Meadow; while in midstream a veritable melee of launches, punts, skiffs and racing eights jostle for position. To add to the confusion you may also encounter a Salter's steamer manoeuvring onto the jetty, this being their upstream terminus. Here also is Salter Bros' island premises and the Head of the River pub. The city centre is only a short walk away.

Bossom's Boatyard

(01865 247780), at Binsey, opposite Port Meadow builds attractive diesel or electric launches and sailing craft. Moorings, Craneage, day hire, engine repairs, brokerage.

Salter Bros. Ltd. (01865 243421). Diesel passenger launch with daily service between Oxford and Abingdon. Craneage and slipway.

Picture: Roy Westlake

The Thames at Folly Bridge, Oxford.